# HOUND DOG

**SINGLES** ▸ A SERIES EDITED BY JOSHUA CLOVER AND EMILY J. LORDI

# HOUND DOG

ERIC WEISBARD

**DUKE UNIVERSITY PRESS** DURHAM AND LONDON 2023

Printed in the United States of America on acid-free paper ∞
Project Editor: Lisa Lawley
Designed by Matthew Tauch
Typeset in Bitter and Work Sans by Copperline Book Services

Library of Congress Cataloging-in-Publication Data
Names: Weisbard, Eric, author.
Title: Hound dog / Eric Weisbard.
Other titles: Singles (Duke University Press)
Description: Durham : Duke University Press, 2023. | Series: Singles | Includes bibliographical references and index.
Identifiers: LCCN 2022055557 (print)
LCCN 2022055558 (ebook)
ISBN 9781478025085 (paperback)
ISBN 9781478020103 (hardcover)
ISBN 9781478027072 (ebook)
Subjects: LCSH: Stoller, Mike. Hound dog. | Stoller, Mike. Hound dog—Adaptations. | Rock music—United States—History and criticism. | Dogs—Songs and music—History—20th century. | BISAC: MUSIC / Genres & Styles / Blues | MUSIC / Genres & Styles / Rock
Classification: LCC ML3534.3 .W467 2023 (print) | LCC ML3534.3 (ebook) | DDC 782.42166—dc23/eng/20230419
LC record available at https://lccn.loc.gov/2022055557
LC ebook record available at https://lccn.loc.gov/2022055558

*This book is dedicated to Frank N. Furter*
*Nietzsche Weisbard, aka Frankie*

*You ain't nothin' but a Maltipoo*

fully knew. My own sense is that musicologist Robert Fink was onto something in comparing the result to "white punk rage—the Ramones, Iggy Pop, the Sex Pistols."[7] Inside the recording tape of that record, where it remained real because it had been preserved but unreal in most other ways (as something that could be spoken about, marketed, straightforwardly codified), the biggest singles artist of the decade, if not all time, had left a premonition of punk on his biggest single. It takes every ounce of Generation X sardonicism I possess not to reach for a Greil Marcus tagline.

Instead, what I'll do in this book is roam around in the singles bin, letting versions and antiversions of "Hound Dog" play out their creation and circulation, with some other dog ditties thrown in for good measure. There's a specific history to dig at here: the birth of a pop singles circuit revved by currents of editable electricity. How that functioned as cultural distortion and feedback, how it was understood in its moment, and how we understand it now can take us through most of the story. We can jump back to minstrelsy and blues, forward to contemplate George Clinton's "Atomic Dog" and DMX's "Get at Me Dog." Patti Page's "Doggie in the Window," scapegoat of every rock and roll history ever, will be explored as one of the genre's key early influences, too popular to be wrong evidence of how studio trickery might stage gaudy unreality. "In other words, I am three," jazz immortal Charles Mingus began his putative memoir, *Beneath the Underdog*, refusing unity in a spirit Black music theorist Fred Moten called, in his trilogy of books, "consent not to be a single being." I cannot treat the Elvis "Hound Dog" single as a single being. Big Mama Thornton beckons. And so does "Doggie."

If this is mainly a story about a dogfight among three categories of music and human being—white woman's pop, Black woman's rhythm and blues, and, finally, white man's rock and roll—at the end we'll revisit that premonition of punk. I never heard an Elvis record as Year Zero. I did feel that way, as a college DJ who became a rock critic, about the Stooges' "I Wanna Be Your Dog." It represented a punk rebellion, sonic as much as social, emerging on singles primarily because they were cheaper to make, an indie label–friendly format, but also because LPs were a rock form and this was as much an antihippie rock and roll restoration as a political act of revolution. The punk single insisted that if a group could make clamor transcendent, who knows what else they—and we—could do. It was a singularity, a scream. And for many of us, listening to an Iggy Pop bellow, or versions like Glenn Danzig in the Misfits and Mark Arm in Mudhoney, then Kurt Cobain in the pop stratosphere, Bikini Kill and Sleater-Kinney subsequently, that yowl was an essence. Where do we put it in our current pop soundscape?

The chapters to come take on "Hound Dog" by exploring why Patti Page was more than whole-fat milk. Why pop through history could be both blackface travesty and sentimental parlor shame. Why Willie Mae Thornton was a groove auteur and not the quintessential Big Black Blues Queen. Why Elvis, extending on Milton Berle's show his bump-and-grind version of a Vegas version of "Hound Dog," ended up in a media cycle that produced a supercharged recording—Screaming White Man—with none of that shimmy. A massive hit single he had to study to learn, scorned in performance, and may even have regretted. How the Berle TV broadcast version was all but lost for rewatching, but the single remained, shaping rock and punk. It's been a long time since we rock and rolled. New acts of restoration, conscious of race and sexuality, are everywhere. But if I am to testify to my own baptism in sound, I need to reflect on the whiteness of the wail.

# ▸01 "Doggie in the Window" and the 1950s Pop Single

**PATTI PAGE'S** "(How Much Is) That Doggie in the Window?" sold millions of copies as a number-one hit in 1953, the year Big Mama Thornton's "Hound Dog" topped the R&B charts. But the dog hit with the cheesy *arf arf*s also became the rock and roll generation's easiest-to-name antithesis, world-threateningly beige like *Invasion of the Body Snatchers* pod people. Bob Dylan, looking back on his childhood in the Cold War era, said, "The music that was popular was 'How Much Is That Doggie in the Window.' That wasn't our reality. Our reality was bleak to begin with. Our reality was fear that at any moment this black cloud would explode."

Dylan took it back on the *Theme Time Radio Hour* he gave to dog songs, if only a bit: "Here's a record that everyone always talks about when they talk about how dull radio was before rock and roll. Personally, I don't agree with them; I think Patti Page made beautiful records." When I played it for Patterson Hood, who leads the quintessential indie version of a southern rock band, Drive-By Truckers, his immediate response was "Thank you, Elvis."[1]

"(How Much Is) That Doggie in the Window?" starts with the soft sound of strings and flutes in a tight, quick measure. Then, just five seconds in, Patti Page sings the chorus. Or Patti Pages: she's multitracked, possible thanks to a very recent technological innovation—magnetic recording. This adds distance, cool of a kind, and the feeling of produced pop: a movie musical reduced a dimension. If we were not already aware of the effects of studio editing, the barks of the doggie in the window—so cute!—highlight that this is a confection. Page's performance luxuriates, drawing chiffon out from her throat. We're in dance time, waltzing along as she narrates a working or at least independent woman's dilemma. "I must take a trip to California." What will become of her "poor sweetheart"? Notice how at this point a muffled string echoes the puppy barks. You couldn't mistake "Doggie" for an art song: each bark, each waggly bit of flute flutter, forbids that. But it expresses affluence and power: a nuclear family forming out in the suburbs perhaps, led by a woman who sounds older than her mid-twenties. And a hint of danger, a threat to that postwar order unrecognized by Dylan in his dismissal of the recording, in a second verse about robbers with flashlights to see in the dark. The doggie will protect her honeybunch from them, too, as much as from his inability to withstand her absence.

Nobody took "Doggie in the Window" seriously. Page, looking back on her career in 1960, wrote, "We thought of it originally as a cute novelty number."[2] But it sold two million copies the first year, then became a children's-record perennial—another expanding segment of a segmenting music industry. As for Page, despite her megahits, the former Clara Ann Fowler of Claremore, Oklahoma, never really received much artistic credit. Few novelty performers, especially women, did, despite the versatility and acumen required of their role.

By contrast, the song Page was most respected for, "Tennessee Waltz," had served a purpose beyond its similar mix of strings, waltz rhythm, and Page harmonizing with herself. The tune, updating the Tin Pan Alley–launching weeper "After the Ball," cemented an alternate publishing powerhouse arriving a half century later. Written by Grand Ole Opry musicians and published by industry leaders Acuff-Rose, "Tennessee Waltz" helped locate Music City as a rival to New York City, with Nashville now the regional center of pop-leaning country music. *Newsweek* would headline an article in 1952 "Country Music Is Big Business, and Nashville Is Its Detroit." This new designation for the "Athens of the South" shifted perceptions. The governor of Tennessee refused to attend the first national Opry broadcast in 1943, calling its music disgraceful. A subsequent governor hurried his ass to Alabama for the funeral of Opry and country legend, not to mention leading Acuff-Rose writer, Hank Williams in early 1953.[3]

Rock and roll hadn't been named in 1953, but pop was already shook up. The two *Billboard* charts renamed in 1949, Rhythm and Blues and Country and Western, reflected genres becoming formats: radio stations, record labels, and associated apparatus. Broadcast Music Incorporated (BMI) handled publishing for writers ASCAP wouldn't touch. The American way prevailed, rival mainstreams at times overlapping, at times very much not.[4] This had little bearing on questions of commerce in music versus art: nobody has ever suggested the criminal-minded owner of Thornton's Peacock Records, Don Robey, was more idealistic than folks at RCA Victor—though Robey did represent the rare presence of a Black label head. What has been presumed, however, is that the indies were more rocking. They were brasher, as a craft-oriented, bureaucratic, major label–ASCAP–Hollywood mindset got replaced by an entrepreneurial, hustling BMI mindset, and that shift extended to the sounds on offer.[5]

This doesn't account for "Doggie in the Window," a decidedly non–rock and roll single produced with entrepreneurial spirit for Mercury Records, an indie started in Chicago in 1945 with an emphasis on jukebox promotion that quickly scaled up its operations. Mercury behaved enough like a major to complicate our ability to fully separate the two categories—which affected the material it sold. In *Race Music*, Guthrie Ramsey looked at the label's first release, "It's Just the Blues," by Four Jumps of Jive—including bassist Willie Dixon, later to write songs for Muddy Waters and Howlin' Wolf that defined Chicago blues. But this "blues-croon," as Ramsey called it, wasn't that pounding style, instead marked by a "subtle criss-crossing of stylistic borders" aimed at cosmopolitan Black Chicagoans with southern roots. Dinah Washington, with her reverse crossover of white hits done blues style for jukeboxes, was a Mercury mainstay. White pop singer Frankie Laine gave the label its first million seller in 1947, helped by Mercury's Mitch Miller, A&R (artist and repertoire) fat cat known for schlocky matches of talent and song. President Berle Adams also managed R&B pioneer Louis Jordan, whose tours were promoted by Thornton's future label boss, Don Robey. Many, many criss-crossings of stylistic borders were in play.[6]

The result was both pop novelties like "Doggie" and a backlash that, as music scholar Keir Keightley has gleefully traced, fully predated rock and roll. A 1948 *Variety* front-pager reported complaints about "'atrocious' melodies." Singer Frank Sinatra complained in 1953, "Trick songs are coming out of my ears." That included, in an RCA Victor A&R man's delineation, "echo chambers, multiple voices, multiple instrumentation, novelty treatment, sexy reading of lyrics, double-entendre lyrics—everything but a solid approach to a solid song as in former years." Here, then, was a category "Doggie" and "Hound Dog" *both* belonged to. Keightley is explicit on Page's number: "Most industry analysts at the time saw it ['Doggie'] as a symptom both of aesthetic decline and of teenage domination of the pop singles chart."[7]

What if the pop singles hated by rock and rollers were made with the same entrepreneurial and indie spirit but just happened to be terrible? Or, at least, something very different from what a tastemaker might esteem? Rebuking the rebukers has been a project of popular music writing for decades now. Steve Waksman, in his study of electric guitar, *Instruments of Desire*, devoted an early chapter to the multitrack pioneer Les Paul, "whose mania is music *delivery systems*," Chet Flippo once noted in *Rolling Stone*. To Waksman, that missed the larger point. Paul was a multiple: "guitarist, inventor, entrepreneur," not to mention a key figure in the domestication of pop, making hits in one of the first home studios with wife Mary Ford, albeit pursuing a white "ideal of tonal purity." "How High the Moon," their 1951 smash, recorded at home, was stereophonic suburban affluence.[8]

Albin Zak's *I Don't Sound Like Nobody* made sound recording the center of 1950s music, with garish peaks of Mitch Miller–approved special effects—Frankie Laine's "Mule Train" whip cracks, Johnnie Ray's sobbing "Cry." The boom in radio stations playing records after World War II included space for Black-oriented stations and DJs who played Black pop to whites. Hits in Nashville were heard in New York. New players followed new pop rules, like Tony Bennett covering Hank Williams at the insistence of his producer, Mitch Miller. For Miller, as for Sam Phillips, the voice coming off the tape was what mattered, plus the sounds dramatizing it.

To singers, though—Page as much as Bennett or Sinatra—the new rules were unsatisfying: they had been raised on jazz standards. Nat Hentoff asked Page, in 1952, "if she were getting tired of all the echo changers and the kinds of songs she has to sing on records." Page said she preferred Ella Fitzgerald and Louis Armstrong, but "the record buying public is mostly composed of the younger people and their interests aren't especially musical when they buy a record." Johnnie Ray, she thought, a boundary blurrer on many levels whose influences included early R&B, was "selling just hysteria. He's not singing." Had she not actually recorded "Doggie in the Window," Page might have been one of its detractors.[9]

Rebuking the rebuker, Zak points out that Page's own more authentic-seeming hit, "Tennessee Waltz," adult target notwithstanding, was no less confected. The 1948 country versions hadn't crossed into pop, so when Mercury wanted a B-side to "Boogie Woogie Santa Claus" for Page, Mercury A&R man Joe Carlton recalled a 1950 cover of "Tennessee Waltz" done for Black listeners and proposed she try one that used some of Erskine Hawkins's trumpet and piano touches: "a pop version of a country song filtered through an R&B cover." In a shook-up pop world, Page's "Doggie" and Presley's and Thornton's "Hound Dog" shared a common recognition: in Zak's words, "making a record meant doing whatever was necessary to breathe life into it."[10]

Other connections emerge when reading Page's memoir, *This Is My Song*. Born in 1927, she called her Oklahoma family "very poor, very large, and very religious"; her mom and older sisters picked cotton. Clara Ann Fowler became Patti Page in high school, singing on KTUL in Tulsa after the family moved to the suburbs and she learned pop from *Song Hits* magazine. One day, "I was told that the girl who was doing the show *Meet Patti Page* sponsored by the Page Milk Company was leaving and asked if I would be interested in being her replacement." At sixteen she did the top-rated show daily at 4:15 p.m., and then she was Ann Foster on *Melody and Stars*, a weekly variety show; duetted on *Five Guys and a Gal*; and sang country on Saturdays with Bob Wills's steel guitarist, Leon McAuliffe. When Jack Rael, road manager for the jazzy Jimmy Joy Orchestra, heard her over the airwaves, she was working with strings and a sax player at a dinner club, too. What cinched the deal was an acetate she mailed him: "He told me once that when he heard my voice again he forgot how I looked." It was 1947, she had a manager in Rael, a label in Mercury, and, as the year came to a close and a recording ban loomed, a new trick: "singing with myself." It was her idea to be what the arrangement for "Confess" called the "echo"—she did it after her A&R man went to the men's room. From that moment, her trademark became the way all the voices on her records fused. Patti Page: creation of milk, acetate, and a bathroom break.[11]

She taught a four-part harmony gimmick to Mitch Miller (though he took credit) for her first million seller and had as fruitful a relationship with Ed Sullivan as the Beatles or Elvis, even guest hosting. "Tennessee Waltz" crossed in many directions, with a *Cashbox* editor teased for thinking a Harlem record store was playing the Erskine Hawkins disc. "Maybe my crossover didn't make waves quite so much as, say, Elvis Presley," Page wrote, but "all musical breakthroughs are important to our culture." Her cohort of female singers included Kay Starr, Georgia Gibbs, Dinah Shore, and friend Rosemary Clooney. She hosted on TV as much as women were allowed: *The Scott Music Hall*, sponsored by a paper company.[12]

Then came "Doggie," title track for the Playcraft children's album *Arfie, the Doggie in the Window*, but the single came out first, so few noticed the likes of "Arfie Catches an Echo." Instead, Page noted, "What everyone who comes to my concerts does remember is that the dog barks on the song because they join in every time!" Elvis got screaming girls; Page got men in the audience making wolf calls and found Homer and Jethro's "(How Much Is) That Hound Dog in the Window" hilarious. She didn't say no to the promotional opportunity to perform "Doggie" on *The Scott Music Hall* but far preferred short films she made as sophisticated openers to the Italian import *Indiscretion of an American Wife*.[13]

Page's personal history was caught up in the social transformations of postwar America—sort of. Brief marriage in 1948 to a well-off man who disappointed her by never working. Introduction to weed in the hotel of a Benny Goodman bandmember. A boyfriend, Joe Guercio, who went from being her piano player/ conductor to playing in Presley's band: "Today he's playing with a projected Elvis onscreen and all the musicians who backed up the King in a great posthumous stage show." Marriage to choreographer Charlie O'Curran; their honeymoon cut short so he could start work on the 1957 Presley picture *Loving You*. The couple worked on separate coasts—red-eye flights weekly. In 1960 she published *Once Upon a Dream: A Personal Chat with All Teenagers*, an "answer" to a similar book by her friend Pat Boone. Presley's mom loved her—when Patti joined Charlie at film shoots, they'd all sing church songs before Elvis left for booty calls. Page and O'Curran adopted Kathleen in Arkansas, went on an extended Asian tour, adopted Danny, stayed on the road. Page anticipated Reba McEntire, wowing critics in *Annie Get Your Gun*; sang with the King of Thailand; charted Easy Listening in her third biz decade with "Gentle on My Mind." One big Tennessee waltz.[14]

She married a final time, at sixty-two, the widower of her best friend. The new couple stepped in during a drug crisis to raise two of their grandkids, the role taking them into their eighties, like a children's record that played forever. Blurring the line between novelties and standards, she rerecorded "Doggie" with the Cincinnati Pops Orchestra for a kids' album, *Young at Heart*. (At Carnegie Hall in 1997, the whole orchestra played the *arfs*.) You can see her old performance clip of it from the once-VHS *The Patti Page Video Songbook*. "It always amazes me how people never forget the old music, particularly 'Doggie in the Window,'" Page wrote. They grew up, she learned, with "a Playcraft record like

'Arfie Goes to the City with Patti Page as Pattibell.'" As in Tinker Bell. "Instead of a fairy with wings, I was depicted on the cover of the record as an angel in an evening gown with a magic wand."[15]

Critic Karen Schoemer attempted to survey the pop *Great Pretenders*, focused on a "tradition of repression and alienation." The first chapter went to Page, who *Down Beat* said in 1950 (as if she was Thornton or Presley) "seems at her best, and her happiest, when she is belting out a blues." In Schoemer's telling, the Page of the late 1990s worried that "cute novelties and pert ditties didn't add up to much." Page said, "the same writer who wrote 'Doggie in the Window' wrote 'People,' if you can imagine. That is a beautiful song that you can put some heart into." Schoemer wanted to object: "Yet it wasn't like I could mount a rousing defense of the social and philosophical significance of 'Doggie in the Window.' Of course it was a silly song." The critic defended the "myth of comfort and serenity that Patti projected," her "strange little snow-globe world."[16] I'd offer one correction. That snow globe wasn't fully Page's—its heart belonged to "Doggie."

True confession time: Back in college, in 1987–88, I wrote a senior thesis with the unfortunate title "Pop Go the Masses," applying what I took to be the viewpoints of different Birmingham Centre for Contemporary Cultural Studies writers to US music from 1954 to 1956. (Hey, it was peak postmodernism.) Rhythm and blues, I thought, resembled Stuart Hall and Tony Jefferson's *Resistance through Rituals*, that first Birmingham collection about working-class subcultures refashioning pop—

sturdy music of the national Other, parallels to Black experience in the United States. Rock 'n' roll, spelled as aggro fans preferred, was like Dick Hebdige's spinoff quickie *Subculture: The Meaning of Style*, allowing in gay punk, bohemia, and the indie ethos of the BBC's John Peel—wild style over lived authenticity. But Hebdige, any cultural studies litany taught, had been devastatingly critiqued by Angela McRobbie's "Settling Accounts with Subculture," which asked why girls having bedroom pop experiences couldn't be as resistant as boys in the street.

That move, too, had a musical parallel. Sure, R&B was an enduring version of independent record label popular music; Elvis Presley at Sun Records in Memphis a full-on rock 'n' roll provocation. But *Billboard* covered another story in those years, just as indie and entrepreneurial—Pat Boone, on the indie label Dot Records, just north of Nashville in Gallatin, Tennessee, mangling Little Richard and Fats Domino to become the *rock and roll* (meeker in spelling and manner than *rock 'n' roll*) star an Elvis fan could tell her parents about.[17] Like the folks who traded favors with Dick Clark in Philly at *American Bandstand*, or like 1970s disco and 1980s MTV later, this indie pop set aside authenticity or resistance. Where did it fit in?

The dilemma, I was trying to say in the ungainly thesis I turned in late and have been futzing with ever since, was that if you accepted the McRobbie critique, if you put a Pat Boone or Patti Page back into the rock and roll story as a full player, then everything was arguably a creative refashioning and no indie subculture should be viewed as implicitly revolutionary. Or at least that's what I thought the dilemma was. Now Hebdige and the concept of the cultural studies academic as cult stud have been roasted in a book, Chris Kraus's *I Love Dick*, reclaiming women's centrality. Stuart Hall's Birmingham writing is used more often to anchor views of Blackness than of bohemia. And rock 'n' roll has become the trickiest of the three modes to celebrate. Which makes Patti Page seem as much a prophet as a one-time source of quick profit. Let the new Bob Dylan Center in Tulsa please heed her call.

# ▸02 Dog Ditties

**THERE'S AN AGE-OLD DISTINCTION,** from sheet music and cheap theater to full-fledged pop, between the minstrel comedy or tearjerker—strange little snow-globe worlds of entertainment genres—and the bluesy embodiment. Contrast Al Bernard's chuckling 1920 vaudeville recording of W. C. Handy's "St. Louis Blues" with the magisterially groove-steeped 1925 disc by Bessie Smith with Louis Armstrong for an idea of what I mean. Or compare Fanny Brice and Billie Holiday versions of "My Man." But don't think that the first mode gets superseded by the second—music roots are far more twisted. It's just a way to listen, to take this story from "Doggie in the Window" (minstrel) to "Hound Dog," and from Big Mama Thornton's "Hound Dog" (blues embodiment) to Elvis Presley's (depends on the version).

As a teaser, consider how even the answer records in between Big Mama and Elvis blur minstrel wink and vernacular swagger. "Bear Cat" by Rufus Thomas, on the same Sun Records that would soon sign Presley, sounds much like Thornton in its delivery, only it answers her back across recordings in what Memphis music later would register as the Otis Redding and Carla Thomas

"Tramp" gender duet on Stax. On the other hand, the joke cover of "Hound Dog" by Freddie Bell and the Bellboys that Presley saw performed live in a Vegas lounge and took to heart is closer to Patti Page material: more recorded *arf arfs*, ethos of the cash-in single. To me, that marks both the Bellboys' "Hound Dog" and Page's "Doggie" as derivations of US pop's first single in spirit: T. D. Rice's 1830s blackface originator and sheet music smash "Jump Jim Crow." Homer and Jethro's "(How Much Is) That Hound Dog in the Window," released on RCA in 1953, when the duo had been signed off the top-tier honkytonk and R&B indie label King Records, provides a true minstrel imprint. Elvis hadn't even visited Sun yet, but RCA was anticipating him, an appropriation impulse we might also connect to the label's other big 1950s profit generator, faux-calypso singer and true political radical Harry Belafonte.

Now rewind a century. In the 1850s, parlor songs included Stephen Foster's "Old Dog Tray," the nation's first successful songwriter getting weepy and cheesy about his faithful companion. Foster, embarrassed by his trashy hits making fun of Black people, sought sentimental alternatives. Blackface minstrelsy and the bourgeois parlor bound together excesses of racism *and* gentility. "Little Old Log Cabin in the Lane," written in the 1870s by one of Foster's successors, William Shakespeare Hays, founded country music when Fiddlin' John Carson recorded it in 1923. Here a white singer voiced in dialect an ex-slave longing for plantation days. *Holiday Inn*, the film that introduced "White Christmas," also had a Bing Crosby blackface scene.[1]

Against this show-business tradition, popular music with rural and urban folk origins asserted group values and a sense of place. Spirituals, the songs of slavery, emerged after the Civil War as a revered tradition, with Fisk University's Jubilee Singers touring worldwide. The Black bandleader W. C. Handy, bringing his troupe to Mississippi, heard amateurs there singing about "going where the Southern cross the Dog," meaning the intersection of two railroads. Stealing the concept for "Yellow Dog Blues," he popularized a genre, the blues, rooted in juke joints across sharecropper towns and city sin streets like Memphis's Beale, Atlanta's Decatur, or New Orleans's Bourbon.[2]

Ultimately, as with Handy, seemingly oppositional musical strands tangled up. Dance styles like ragtime and jazz had elements of classical music orchestration. Touring medicine shows were permeated with coon song caricature even while introducing such blues singers as Ma Rainey and Bessie Smith. And records made it unnecessary for a listener to have proximity to a performer. Consider "Crazy Blues," written by Perry Bradford and recorded by Mamie Smith and Her Jazz Hounds in 1920. Was it blues or jazz or both? And who let the hounds in? Bradford, a veteran of Decatur Street relocated to New York, didn't care, nor did the vaudeville singer, Smith. But African American listeners, sold the record by Pullman porters hauling it nationally, took pride in the first Black pop music record. When some of those listeners favored more "down-home" singers, like the solo guitarist Blind Lemon Jefferson, companies sent units south to record them in bulk.[3]

By the end of the 1920s, a multifaceted pop music industry had formed. Duke Ellington, ensconced at the segregated Cotton Club, still connected to the Harlem Renaissance through records, radio broadcasts, and even short films. Hollywood musicals, sparked by Al Jolson in blackface as *The Jazz Singer*, demanded new material: the previous century's minstrelsy-parlor combo swelled into a jazz–Tin Pan Alley alliance of rhythm and love songs, novelty lyrics and lasting standards. Radio networks made crooners into stars, with a Nashville station, WSM, premiering the old-time variety show *Grand Ole Opry*, airing weekly for almost a century now. Jimmie Rodgers, merging Fiddlin' John Carson and Mamie Smith with his "blue yodels," became a roots superstar, duetting with Louis Armstrong. The 78 RPM discs sounded better than before, as electrical recording replaced an acoustic that required theatrical bluster. An international cavalcade resulted, from South American tango to Egyptian diva Umm Kulthum.[4]

Record sales were then devastated by the Depression, resulting in a tighter mainstream, a radical underground, and a reliance on youth culture. Now a figure like Crosby could become a star of radio, screen, and records all at once. But even Crosby needed "Brother, Can You Spare a Dime?," an anthem of economic hardship, to make clear he wasn't just a frivolous celebrity.

Popular culture became a place for performers to ask, as in the protest song popularized by Pete Seeger and Woody Guthrie's Almanac Singers, "Which Side Are You On?" Gospel quartets, inheritors of the spirituals legacy, headlined union rallies. Billie

Holiday sang an antilynching song written by a member of the Communist Party: "Strange Fruit," released on an independent record label and performed at New York's left-wing, integrated Café Society. Popular Front culture, including musicals like Marc Blitzstein's *The Cradle Will Rock*, used songs, dance, and the like to make proletarian statements.[5]

It was radicalism of a different sort when a football stadium's worth of young jitterbugs gathered in Chicago in 1938 for a full day of swing dancing to an integrated lineup of musicians. Only three years earlier, Chicago-raised Benny Goodman and his band, who specialized in the hot arrangements club owners were convinced didn't sell, found a surprisingly big audience in Los Angeles, where fans got to hear the group's live network-radio broadcasts hours earlier than their late-night placement elsewhere. At the Palomar Ballroom, a swing generation announced itself. Fans were part of the first national cohort to all attend high school, as peer culture solidified. Avid New Dealers, they identified with Goodman, a child of Jewish immigrants who made part of his otherwise all-white Orchestra engagements a set-apart mixed-race quartet. Swing groups turned the sounds of Louis Armstrong into a nationally understood pop undercurrent. Records boomed again, heard on jukeboxes that encouraged common listening and accessible sounds, like Ella Fitzgerald and Chick Webb's "A-Tisket, A-Tasket." Soon a new term took hold: the *teenager*.[6]

Frank Sinatra reshaped American music stardom by drawing on all this. A child of immigrants, too, in his case Italians, he emerged singing with a white swing band, led by Tommy Dorsey, then sang pop smashes of the day on the first show devoted to the topic, radio's *Your Hit Parade*. Declared unfit for combat during World War II, Sinatra went solo, his 1944 appearances at Brooklyn's Paramount Theatre treated with such girlish passion that he was nicknamed "Swoonatra." But Sinatra, new symbol of mainstream pop, idol of youth culture, was also outspoken politically. *The House I Live In*, a short film from 1945, showed him confronting anti-Semitism and singing the title song about America as ideally a land of tolerance, lyrics by the author of "Strange Fruit."[7]

The war sent rural people, especially Black and white southerners, to cities for defense work and armed service; money coursed again, feeding a new version of the 1920s old-time and blues categories. Country music became honkytonk, hits like "Walking the Floor Over You" and "Pistol Packin' Mama" taking on electrification and a new lyrical freedom. And down-home blues were amplified by guitar greats such as T-Bone Walker and Muddy Waters. Gospel boomed, too, with figures like Mahalia Jackson emerging as culture heroes. Small record labels catered to the new sounds: a parallel music industry.[8]

The postwar United States was more prosperous economically and less tolerant politically. With Joseph McCarthy and the House Un-American Activities Committee leading a Red Scare, anybody viewed as socialist came under subpoena, and culture was scrutinized closely. The lines complaining about private-property signs in Woody Guthrie's folksy national anthem "This

Land Is Your Land" were no longer sung. But popular music rang the register, putting new kinds of voices, however regulated, into the public sphere. Rebellion was personalized, coded, sonic; generational or regional or racial or bohemian; not rhetorically collective and clear.[9]

The splintering of mass culture first evident with old-time and race records in the 1920s and swing youth culture in the 1930s now became an aggressive segmentation. Television, the big media-technology story of the 1950s, took the syndicated network shows off radio. Many programmers responded with a Top 40 hits format for kids or easy listening sounds aimed at housewives. Also broken apart was the jazz-Broadway-Hollywood alliance that had nurtured Armstrong, Crosby, and Sinatra. Big bands were declared unsustainable: a better economy meant musicians wanted higher pay; singers were increasingly dominant; and live amplification joined to magnetic recordings let smaller combos sound almost as versatile. Jazz developed a modernist subculture, bebop. The jump blues of Louis Jordan, New Orleans piano rhythms by Fats Domino, replaced swing as dance beats.[10]

It wasn't just a new singer in the Sinatra style, Tony Bennett, whose label boss, Mitch Miller, made him record tunes he categorically despised. Sinatra himself, subject to Miller's song choices after his career foundered in the early 1950s, complained even more loudly, telegramming a congressional committee years later that Miller had forced him to make "many,

many inferior songs." Yet another dog number, "Mama Will Bark," a duet with busty comedienne Dagmar, has often been called the worst recording of Sinatra's career. His departure from Columbia Records for Capitol, where he concentrated on albums, not singles, and exerted control over his repertoire, can be understood as stemming from the desire to get as far away from Mitch Miller as possible.[11]

So, to review: American popular music, as show-business entertainment, relied on doggone dubious origins: racist blackface minstrelsy, weepy bourgeois parlor songs. Genres of music like blues, jazz, gospel, and country asserted a counterpressure: they were more rooted in places, people, and specific sounds. But in a mass culture of records, radio, movies, and now TV, you couldn't separate the fake from the real: it all mixed together. Different eras did have different forces at work, however. In affluent, anticommunist postwar America, that meant hostility toward overt Depression-style populism, yet also the prosperity to support a wider range of voices and styles so long as what they supplied was more signifier, punctum, effect than outright messaging. Rock and roll was the loudest result, almost noisy enough to cover over its patched-together beginnings.

# 03 "Hound Dog," Take One: Big Mama Thornton

**LISTENING TO THE ORIGINAL "HOUND DOG,"** we're in a different sonic universe than in "Doggie in the Window," as Big Mama Thornton's rumbling, phlegmy, and oratorical voice gets the support of what will soon become understood as rock rather than jazz backing: electric guitar, bass, and drums. The beat, slinky more than driving, steeps in atmospherics. Thornton, supplying howls to go with an instrumental break that lasts more than a third of the song, bodies up to the sound. It's musical worldmaking, studio-edited cabaret. Here, too, there are barks at the end. But one is as likely to notice Thornton's shifting vocal accents, or the Latin rhythms—a *Switched on Pop* podcast episode identified it as the *tresillo*, bumping from Cuban *contradanza* to New Orleans Mardi Gras—that the Puerto Rican–born bass player insinuated. "Sex," Patterson Hood of the Drive-By Truckers said to me after this one played. "Dirty sex."[1]

In the classic origin story of rock and roll, postwar youth were given the choice between Page milk and Thornton whiskey and chose intoxication over pasteurization. Even cover versions, like Pat Boone ripping off Little Richard, or Georgia Gibbs duplicating LaVern Baker, proved a passing phase—rock and rollers over time helped define themselves by embracing the Black originators. But that ignores the vastly more prominent Elvis Presley "Hound Dog" or the reason Thornton never got paid for "Hound Dog," never had a second hit, but did see a second number, "Ball and Chain," eclipsed by another white rocker, Janis Joplin. This, then, has become the classic rock and roll revisionist story: Black music, especially as performed by Black women, was buried by white rock's self-serving mythology and now sorely needs reclamation.

I have no totalizing statement to put up against these two powerhouse tales, just a lifelong dropping of the jaw at the way pop history, the longer we spend with it, dispels certainty. Let me lay out the fuller list of particulars—telling details and mixed repertoire. Those are not insignificant. Let's see where they lead.

Of the cast in the initial production, Mike Leiber and Jerry Stoller were white Jewish songwriters, both just nineteen and starting out. They met in Los Angeles, bonded over their love of Black music, and found it possible to get their songs recorded in the newly named music industry category of rhythm and blues. Willie Mae Thornton, then twenty-five, was from Alabama, singing in both churches and traveling revues, where her bluesy growl earned comparisons to Bessie Smith. In Houston she signed to Peacock Records, one of the few labels owned and run by an African American, Don Robey, forty-eight, also a club and booking agency owner. Drummer and bandleader Johnny Otis, thirty, born Ioannis Alexandres Veliotes to Greek immigrant parents, had—in his mind—rhetorically switched races, writing later, "As a kid I decided that if our society dictated that one had to be black or white, I would be black."[2]

This was not utter white appropriation. That came later. Yet issues of identity and authorship shaped how "Hound Dog" came to exist and who ultimately cashed in—we can't just say, "It's complicated" as if assessing a new relationship on Facebook. Clearly, race was already in play—loud play. "Hound Dog," commissioned by Robey and Otis to give Thornton her first hit, was a cross-racial production made in common testament to Black-identified blues, created in a studio environment, for sale to what was presumed to be a Black audience, and with the most initial power held by Robey, known for ruthless business practices.

Just as much at stake in each sung "You ain't nothing but" were notions of gender and class. Where Page bought a puppy, Thornton, in full-on attack mode as she named her man a no-good dog, embodied what Jack Halberstam has called "female masculinity." As Maureen Mahon puts it, she "flouted the expectations of dominant black and white middle-class arbiters of propriety," wearing men's clothing onstage, though her private sexuality remains unknown. Mahon notices how Thornton bosses her guitarist on the track. Wag, she tells him.[3]

The issue of authorship has related complexities. Thornton didn't author "Hound Dog" in the sense that steers copyright law, derived from Tin Pan Alley, ASCAP, and sheet music. In the minstrel and vaudeville tradition of show business that predated recordings and movies, songs came first, and "pluggers" hired by publishers coaxed singers to add them to their act, the earliest payola. Theatrical songs were sentimental, not personal, though sentiments ranged from comic to teary and became more urbane over time. Notably, the name of ASCAP's eventual competitor, BMI, founded in 1939, stood for Broadcast Music, Inc. Radio strained the earlier system. As listeners fell in love with soft-toned heartbreakers, crooners and torch singers escaped from side positions in bands and orchestras to become stars. Just as the studio concoction "Doggie in the Window" was seemingly the opposite of rock and roll but appeared an identical crass novelty to traditionalists, "sweet music" threatened taste before electrified R&B and honkytonk used radio to deliver rougher voices.[4]

Thornton knew that while the "Hound Dog" copyright belonged to others, she had a vernacular claim: it was nothing without her tone, her act. She told critic Ralph Gleason, "I started to sing the words and I put in some of my own. All that talkin' and hollerin', that's my own."[5] Thornton grew up outside Montgomery, Alabama, with a preacher dad and a choir singer mom, learning harmonica and drums from brother "Harp" Thornton. Adrift after her mother died of tuberculosis, she went from cleaning a tavern to rocking it. Diamond Teeth Mary (McClain) heard her singing on a garbage truck and told her about a contest, and she won it. Thornton joined Sammy Green's Hot Harlem Revue at fourteen, alongside Little Richard, who, Thornton's biographer tells us, said that with few exceptions "everybody on his [Green's] show was a sissy." Tall and a growler, Thornton was billed as the new Bessie Smith. In Atlanta the revue played the 81 Bailey Theatre on Decatur Street, where Smith emerged as a 1910s teen and Thomas Dorsey, not yet father of gospel, had been a "butch boy" selling soda and popcorn while cadging musical tips. Thornton, a generation later, paid badly by the troupe, shined shoes in front of the entrance.[6]

Big Mama's musical performances epitomized a specific tradition. In the great history *Jazz Dance*, Birmingham's Leola B. Wilson recalled the action in her father's honkytonk. "I remember a tall, powerful woman who worked in the mills pulling coke from a furnace—a man's job. It was Sue, and she loved men. When Sue arrived at my father's honky tonk, people would yell: 'Here come Big Sue! Do the Funky Butt, Baby!' As soon as she got high and happy, that's what she'd do, pulling up her skirts and grinding her rear end like an alligator crawling up a bank." As historian Tera Hunter sums up, "The major underlying principles that informed the blues aesthetic and [were] embodied in vernacular dance were irreverence, transcendence, social realism, self-empowerment, and collective individualism." Thornton fit that index. She sang, she blew harp, she played drums, she told jokes—her presence was the act you could not follow.[7]

Thornton originated "Hound Dog" at the beginning of an era that would insist that the best songs were not novelties or standards passed around between entertainers but the recorded work of a single artist in a single moment, putting something of who they were into the grooves. Popular music iconicity stopped centering as much on a song becoming a widespread smash on many a stage and looked to star texts like Billie Holiday's *Lady Sings the Blues*, to genres, scenes, and subcultures that gave recordings a pop version of folkloric place.

That connected perfectly with talent scout and bandleader Johnny Otis, the farthest thing from a cultural imperialist but a presentational maven nonetheless. Otis started the Barrelhouse Club in the Black Los Angeles neighborhood Watts in 1948, possibly the first club to specialize in R&B, then the Johnny Otis Rhythm and Blues Caravan. He'd have fifteen R&B hits between 1950 and 1952, as well as staging integrated concerts in El Monte's Legion Stadium after LA police drove him from the city. Ethnic studies scholar George Lipsitz told the story of "Pachuco Hop," where "the first L.A. Chicano rock and roll star turned out to be a Hungarian Jew, produced and promoted by a Greek who thought of himself as Black!" Otis would go on to politics and author a book about the Watts riots, would host programs that made radio a ritual space for Blackness. At Thornton's funeral, Otis gave the eulogy, thinking, Lipsitz wrote, "about how lucky he had been to know her, to be part of the community that she came out of, and to be involved with the people he saw at her funeral. Music had made it possible for him to learn about African American culture and to fight for it."[8]

Less idealistic than Otis, but no less zealous about defining his turf, was Peacock Records owner Robey, who wrote and played nothing but kept most of the money. Was he a "Hound Dog" author, too, for making a space the song could launch from, a less admirable version of Motown's own sharp Black business owner, Berry Gordy, or the precursor to Death Row Records' Suge Knight? Robey, who got his start running joints in Houston, had booked elegant Black swing bands before the war, then recalibrated to launch Louis Jordan's jump blues as a live draw—early R&B shows. As Preston Lauterbach tells it, "Robey had become part of a fraternity of light-skinned kingpins like himself whose membership spanned the South. They all ran nightclubs rife with gambling, liquor, prostitution—or all of the above. At the national level, these playboys were the backbone of the black entertainment industry known as the chitlin' circuit. Robey and his colleagues operated in a shadow world, segregated from white society just as black music was segregated from mainstream pop in the r&b category."[9] Robey sold his companies in 1973 for a reported million dollars.

Thornton was at home in the world Robey bankrolled, Otis sought to redeem, and Leiber and Stoller sampled. Evelyn Johnson, who ran Buffalo Booking, Peacock's boutique chitlin circuit, described her as a "female thug": "She was very blunt, and she used a lot of bad language. She wore khaki pants, plaid shirts, all the time." But that's what Johnson and Robey liked about her—that and her ability to appeal outside the South, to blow Little Esther off the stage of Harlem's Apollo Theater, the very moment Willie Mae was renamed Big Mama. An ad Robey took out called her a "House Rocker and Show Stopper."[10]

Which brings us back to the rock and roll question: house rocker? *Rock* meaning what? Leiber and Stoller's joint memoir was titled *Hound Dog* because Nesuhi Ertegun had said, "'Gentlemen . . . you'll always be remembered as the guys who wrote 'Hound Dog.'" That "gentlemen, be seated" note, from minstrelsy, was appropriate: these were two Jews putting on Blackness. Stoller made much of hearing boogie-woogie at age eight at a radical New Jersey sleepaway camp, where he acquired the contacts to check out bebop in Harlem. Leiber had Dunbar, "a black dude who taught me," and cited "Doggie" as an example of a record that "drove me crazy. I stuck my fingers in my ears to get away from that crap." He bonded with Stoller writing blues songs: "When Jerry sang, he sounded black," Stoller reported, while Stoller had the James P. Johnson piano moves. Jimmy Witherspoon recorded their "Real Ugly Woman," including the lyric "she's 300 pounds of meat and she's my female Frankenstein." Thornton was that last metaphor personified, so far as Leiber and Stoller were concerned. In their memoir, they call her "frightening" in her "combat boots and oversized overalls," a force of nature "monstrous" but right for "deadly blues." This Big Mama pointed at her crotch, told Leiber, "Attack this." Stoller said, "It was as much her appearance as her blues style that influenced the writing of 'Hound Dog.'" Otis vented about the duo, "They had some derogatory crap. I constantly had to edit their songs."[11]

Then again, Leiber and Stoller might reply, Otis had played his position as a radio show host for plenty of laughs. The man Lipsitz called "Southern California's most recognizable representation of Black music" put what singer Etta James called his "jivetime jazzman's voice, but it's also sincere and full of wisdom" in comic dialogue with foil Redd Foxx. Otis was both the political force who had a cross burned on his lawn and the man who put out an album called *Snatch and the Poontangs*. He loved Thornton, but he also depicted her drinking a combo of grape juice and embalming fluid, one of those "wild women don't have the blues" caricatures.[12]

Rock meaning what? Leiber and Stoller and Otis alike, I'd argue, missed a rocking side of Thornton worth describing not as superhuman bluster but as literary and auteurist, narrating fiercely and, in singing terms, intellectually from within the mix. Akin to W. C. Handy, Mamie Smith, and countless other maintainers of the genre-crazy blues. Able to assert performance artistry with a signature style that revealed the limits of *both* sheet-music-business urbanity and folkloric mythology. And particularly well suited for the rock and roll moment when records became mini-movies, short stories, dramatic tales in three minutes. I want to make this thesis cross-racial, too. Thornton *and* Presley, Louis Armstrong and Hoagy Carmichael before them, Bob Dylan and Aretha Franklin after them, through to maybe Miley Cyrus and Lizzo right now, loved all kinds of music and—this is critical—especially loved to reauthor it, using such techniques as tribute bordering on travesty, collage that courted charges of plagiarism, meme and variation. That's what lurks in "Hound Dog." Literary or auteurist musicking, to call up Christopher Small's phrase, ushers us through a song; it doesn't seek to be some wild thing. Even as R&B or rock and roll, it's on par with, not opposed to, Leiber and Stoller's subsequent revamping of German literature as Anglo-American cabaret, their hit with Peggy Lee, "Is That All There Is?"[13]

Consider as evidence another number you could write a book about. From my punk and indie perspective, an intriguing detail in Thornton's one biography is that on October 3, 1981, she played a show in Los Angeles at a club called Lingerie with none other than the Gun Club. What a forgotten rock moment! But if we want pop's striations to map themselves into our skull, move ahead to July 1984, when on her last day alive she gathered some friends, called her sister Mattie, and "sang for her, her favorite song 'That Lucky Old Sun.'"[14]

The standard is arguably a poor relation of "Ol' Man River," that white-authored song of Black suffering and the world's indifference, alchemized in *Show Boat* by Paul Robeson, though Robeson was backed on the first recording by Paul Whiteman and his white-man orchestra.[15] "That Lucky Old Sun" salutes the ball in the sky for lazing while folks like the singer work. The first to hit with it was Frankie Laine, steered by Mitch Miller—yes, "Lucky Old Sun" comes from the breeding grounds of "Doggie in the Window." It's pop-schlock, southern style—Beasley Smith, who did the music, became staff arranger for inglorious Dot Records. Smarmy baritone Vaughn Monroe competed with Laine in the charts. Frank Sinatra held his nose and put a version in the competition. Still, Louis Armstrong was in the pop battle, too, and crooner Herb Lance (later to co-write "Mama, He Treats Your Daughter Mean" for Ruth Brown) brought "Lucky" into the R&B charts. Ray Charles, in the film *Ballad in Blue*, performed it for somber white people. Sammy Davis Jr., on his *Impersonating* album, covers it in the voices of Laine, Charles, and Ellington singer Al Hibbler. Others amped the seriousness: Brian Wilson worked with Van Dyke Parks on a concept album around it; Willie Nelson and Johnny Cash brought austerity to their renderings, creating a country lineage that Kenny Chesney was happy to claim for white populism.[16]

Thornton's version of "That Lucky Old Sun" appeared on the 1969 Mercury album *Stronger Than Dirt*, alongside new versions of "Hound Dog" and "Ball and Chain," George Gershwin's "Summertime," Muddy Waters' "Rollin' Stone," Albert King via Stax's "Born Under a Bad Sign," her old labelmate Bobby Bland's "Ain't Nothin' You Can Do," the Ashford & Simpson–written (for the Coasters, then Ronnie Milsap, but most prominently performed by Ray Charles) "Let's Go Get Stoned," and the Dylan song "I Shall Be Released." Her "Lucky" in 1969 shared something rare, from what I've heard, with the one Dylan recorded for an album of standards associated with Frank Sinatra, *Shadows in the Night*. Thornton and Dylan put aside personalizing the song, didn't bother making it their own. They diffused the performance into multiplicities of cultural categories. Became their own backing chorus, redeeming clichés. But listeners could still hear their authorship.

Admirers have been trained to recognize Dylan's lovely thefts as desubjectification, an artistic move renouncing countercultural authenticity as he once spurned protest songs. In *Chronicles*, he watched Frank Sinatra Jr. at the Rainbow Room, preferring that to being designated the "Big Bubba" of cultural heroics by old Left poet Archibald MacLeish or his too-earnest rock band compadre Robbie Robertson. Thornton, his fellow harmonica enthusiast and comedian, brought similar restlessness to her belated major-label album release. Nat Dove, pianist on the session, said she "wanted it to sound as good as possible, but she wanted it to be not so structured. She had some arranges on it too." A *New York Times* review by Don Heckman credited this "appropriately eclectic program" to producer Al Schmitt but said she was best doing blues; a *Rolling Stone* review by John Morthland said Schmitt "and arrangers Rene Hall and Everett Minor really got carried away with their jobs, and have almost bled Big Mama's music of the drive and spontaneity that are her trademarks."[17] An artistry "not so structured" is a trickier one to celebrate than "drive and spontaneity" posited as innate power supply, but to my ears it's Thornton's authority within "Hound Dog," not a reductive association of Black women's vernacular with premodern primitivism.

Janis Joplin had a bigger hit singing "Ball and Chain" than Thornton ever did, her second pilfering by a white performer, yet Joplin credited Thornton, performed with her, got her some royalties. Still, what we might call the Both/And story goes beyond that. Both/And was the name of the San Francisco club, on Divisadero Street (one of the many Black music streets ripped away by so-called urban renewal), where Joplin and another Big Brother cofounder, James Gurley, heard Thornton perform "Ball and Chain." Gurley: "I said to Janis afterward: 'You know we could rearrange that song.' It was in a major key, kind of an up-tempo thing the way she did it. I said: 'We could put it in a minor key and slow it down and make it a heavier song." And so they did. Gurley again: "I don't want to be a re-creator. I want to be a creator."[18]

Much revisionism around Big Mama Thornton's both/and place in music history has aimed to afford her the same position: rearranger as creator. Tyina Steptoe, considering Thornton alongside Little Richard, turns Johnson's "female thug" into emblematic "gender nonconformity." As the two moved from the safer spaces, in some ways, of traveling troupes to pursue a mass market, they had to "dilute the queer content of their performances." Steptoe comments on Thornton's tie-and-trousers look, her Black male conk hairstyle, her rejection in "No Jody for Me" of the "backdoor man" looking for money from married ladies.[19]

Kimberly Mack's *Fictional Blues* compares Thornton to Shug Avery in Alice Walker's *The Color Purple*, equating literary figures and constructed personas. Thornton bridges Bessie Smith to Amy Winehouse, offering "unconventional autobiographical performances" to take back her work. Maureen Mahon writes, "In many popular music histories, Thornton has been reduced to a symbol: the ripped-off African American musician on whose unacknowledged shoulders subsequent generations of rock and rollers stand." For Mahon and Mack, the goal is to not just restore Thornton's position but complicate it. Even Michael Spörke's less critically complicated account has a revealing gig moment, where Thornton tells her hired drummer, in front of the audience, how to play "Hound Dog" in "the Big Mama Way." Tom Principato, another musician that night, said, "I did have the impression, though, that this was not the first time this had happened between Big Mama and a drummer, and that Big Mama used it as part of her show. Quite a grand finale. Big Mama was a pretty good drummer, too."[20]

As I write this book, Thornton's "Hound Dog" can be heard sampled within "Vegas," made for Baz Luhrmann's biopic *Elvis*, by Los Angeles–raised rapper-singer Doja Cat. In the film you see a quick version by an actress with gospel chops, playing at Club Handy on Beale Street; that merges into the Doja Cat track in the first of Luhrmann's deliberate mash-ups of past and present. We can do the same with Doja Cat herself, viewing her as a true heir to the polyglot 1953 recording team. She was born Amala Ratna Zandile Dlamini in 1995 to a Jewish-American graphic designer mom and a South African performer dad who had appeared in the musical *Sarafina!* She spent time growing up at a commune founded by jazz's Alice Coltrane. Doja, sampler of "Hound Dog," earlier found homology with the Page Milk Company, namers of Patti, when she became popular with "Mooo!" That began, "Bitch I'm a cow / I'm not a cat, I don't say meow"; dairily invoked Wu-Tang Clan's "C.R.E.A.M."; and ended with a big nod to "Milkshake," by another half-lost figure, singer Kelis. Checking boxes, Doja Cat later covered Hole's grunge–meets–Hot AC classic "Celebrity Skin."

Literary and auteurist musickers, shaking up a new century. As an audio recording, "Vegas" gives us Doja the "bad bitch" dog, with Thornton's "you ain't nothing but a . . ." a valediction, though where Big Mama growled, Doja Cat jabs, like role model Nicki Minaj; girlish sweetness adroitly queered. (*Switched on Pop*'s hosts noted that the *tresillo* beat, back in vogue in the 2020s in the likes of Jack Harlow's "Dua Lipa" and Bad Bunny merengue updates, was prominent once again in this track, after diminishing but not disappearing in the Presley cover.)[21] But for the accompanying music video, Luhrmann's vision of pop as a *Moulin Rouge*–meets–*Gatsby* cabaret sequence dominates: the camera is consumed gazing at his pseudo-Elvis, conveying snip by snip how a seizure of the Black evangelical tent-show variety became the King's screaming, shaking reaction. The film itself presents Colonel Parker, Presley's longtime manager, in something of the way I have presented Don Robey: the show-business hustler with the criminal con as a figure of not so much rock and roll, or R&B, as extreme pop—the carnival and the slot machine.

*Elvis*, after those sizzling seconds of the actress playing Thornton as a torch singer (Shonka Dukureh, found dead in her Nashville home at age forty-four just weeks after the film debuted), comes closest to the idea of Black women creating rock and roll via current singer Yola as Sister Rosetta Tharpe, singing "Strange Things Happening Every Day." But Tharpe's title reinforces the idea of show business as topsy-turvy, centering Luhrmann's pop-art cosmology, not delivering a message of reparations. Back on the Doja Cat single, a recurring sample of Thornton, or perhaps it's Dukureh, or it could be a blend (recording having gone from electric to digital to deep fake), begs, nay screams, to differ from all this implacable marginalizing. "You ain't nothing," she berates . . . Presley? Luhrmann? Even now, there is no Elvis without her.

# ▸ 04 Elvis Presley Belatedly Records "Hound Dog"

**TWO TIDBITS.** In one, Big Mama Thornton is talking Elvis Presley in 1971: "Well, he refused to play with me when he first come out and got famous. They wanted a big thing for Big Mama Thornton and Elvis Presley. He refused, and I'm so glad I can tell the world about it." In another, Scotty Moore, Presley's first guitarist, emails Thornton's biographer to say that the not-yet-king did seek out her sometime musical partner Johnny Ace as 1954 became 1955: "As it happened, he was dead before we arrived, but Elvis and I went to the venue where Johnny Ace had died and were shown the dressing room where it happened." We also learn that Moore had then in his possession Presley's original 78 RPM version of Thornton's "Hound Dog."[1]

Was Elvis coldhearted, misdirected, compartmentalized, canny? Our remaining questions can't be easily answered. But Presley found something in the Freddie Bell Las Vegas cover version he could work with, unlike Thornton's, starting with making a song about a no-good woman-chasing man into a song about a no-good rabbit-chasing canine. He incorporated "Hound Dog" into live shows, the response so dramatic that when he returned to Milton Berle's TV program the unrecorded number spawned a national controversy. Presley, fronting a trio of drums, electric guitar, and bass, was in motion within seconds: swivel hips that older jazz fans could date back but kids considered the most sexual thing they'd been allowed to see. The music, arranged like Bell's version, kept some of the guitar flash of Thornton's. But there was only a brief instrumental break. Instead, the sex part continued as the song repeated. And now the camera turned to white girls stirring. Ninety seconds in, "Hound Dog" was done. But Presley's band slowed to a bump and grind for another thrusting minute—Patterson Hood, watching the clip, goggled. "If Big Mama was a hand grenade," he mused, "this was an atomic bomb."[2]

"Hound Dog" didn't instantly register as transgressive on the show. Berle pretended to ruin his shoes with a comic imitation of Presley's moves. Then he talked with Presley about the girls "flipping their lids" and mimicked them as well, familiar territory from Frank Sinatra's day. A starlet came out to scream on cue. Berle alluded to both "Blue Suede Shoes" and "Heartbreak Hotel," the hits Presley had performed on his first appearance. Later in the program, the host had a seven-year-old perform "Heartbreak Hotel."

The media response wasn't laughing, denouncing "primitive physical movement difficult to describe in terms suitable to a family newspaper" and "'grunt and groin' antics." Rock and roll, controversial for race mixing and an air of juvenile delinquency, now had a sex symbol, though Presley said it was "just my way of expressing how I feel when I move around." He told the *Charlotte Observer*, "Them critics don't like to see nobody win doing any kind of music they don't know nothing about." And he was clear on that ignorance. "The colored folks been singing it and playing it just like I'm doin' now, man, for more years than I know. They played it like that in the shanties and in their juke joints, and nobody paid it no mind 'til I goosed it up."[3]

What followed should have damned American entertainment as smothering balderdash. *Tonight Show* host Steve Allen said, "If he does appear, you can rest assured that I will not allow him to do anything that will offend anyone." A bewildered Presley donned black tie and tails, so Allen could compliment him on his presentability. Then he sang a crooner's number, succeeding in a style his rock and roll was rendering passé. Allen next brought on stage a basset hound, seemingly medicated. Presley performed "Hound Dog" to the creature, sex drained out. That still wasn't enough. Summoned back, he appeared with Allen in a "western" sketch, actually a minstrel sketch: the first tune heard was "Turkey in the Straw," aka "Zip Coon."[4]

The next day, Presley recorded his much punkier version of "Hound Dog." As biographer Peter Guralnick documents, fans outside the building held signs like "We Want the GYRATIN' Elvis." This would be a good second moment to consider the Baz Luhrmann biopic *Elvis*, where those fans are relocated to outside Graceland, and the decision to rock out once and forever to the evening, two days later, on July 4, when Presley performed in Memphis to fourteen thousand Black and white youths, including the promise that "those people in New York are not gonna change me none," even as on that same day Mississippi senator James Eastland told 3,500 Memphians in Overton Park two miles over, "Proponents of desegregation really are after racial amalgamation, and we in the South aren't going to stand for it." It was a historic contrast: Michael Bertrand makes that Independence Day central to the conclusion of his book *Race, Rock, and Elvis*.[5] The Luhrmann film gives us this seemingly staged, actually true contrast. But it gives us seemingly true, actually false details imported from other shows, too. It rushes by and won't fully differentiate, leaving the audience that work. Like "Hound Dog." Like a lot of rock and roll.

Luhrmann understands the importance of singles: one of the first scenes has Colonel Parker hearing Presley for the first time, the record "That's All Right"; he's shocked to learn that Presley is white. In another scene, the inducted King courts Priscilla by playing her some of his 45s. This conceptually jam-packed film gives us quick glimpses of Presley in the Sun and RCA studios, trying with fitful results to get his sound across. There is a moment where we see him orchestrating a Vegas version of "That's All Right." The Elvis who wiggled is fully preserved in *Elvis*: the Berle show; the Allen humiliation, turning Presley into a "butler." Even Parker is portrayed as liking the wiggle, which he says is a "snow job" just like his merchandising hustles, at least until the outrage gets too fierce and he advocates limited family entertainment. *Elvis* the movie rests on the notion that Presley's life and art remained eternally precarious, save perhaps for his love of Black gospel and blues first, romancing of female listeners second.

The biopic, for all its reenactments, fails to put us inside the studio on the day "Hound Dog" was recorded. On that day Elvis was at last in charge, and the results were fierce and firm—different from the Black music he loved or the sexy performance style he stroked his fans with. Eighteen takes made the rhythm harder. Thirty-one takes in, they stopped. Coupled as a single with "Don't Be Cruel," this version dominated the charts, a record then for eleven weeks at number one. He closed his shows with it, introducing it as the "Elvis Presley national anthem."[6]

Did Presley coauthor this "Hound Dog," as many would argue that Thornton had? His voice roars out to start, the growl reverbed to resonate. The sound separations—backing vocals, glimmers of electric guitar, lively bass, clapped beats—mix into a new rhythm:

jetting rather than atmospheric, diminishing the *tresillo* rhythm effect. With the gender battle and in-concert sex play deleted, the song becomes a class battle: "They said you was high-classed / Well, that was just a"—line? Lie? On a record we can't see the hips move, can't endure a staging with a dull-eyed dog. We compensate, hear the swivel in how he just slightly pauses to signify on his own vocal rhythm about thirty-five seconds in, on what's already his fourth sung "You ain't . . ." (not even counting those thirty earlier takes, the live versions, the TV remakes). Nothing is comic here, à la the Freddie Bell version. Wild: a guitar chord that sounds willfully mishit, the Jordanaires putting one flat note up against the sparks in Scotty Moore's note runs. Pounding: the claps in particular. Angry: an emotion that lurked every time he called Steve Allen or Milton Berle "sir." But not minstrel.

The twenty-one-year-old Presley, spending hours in the studio, recorded in a manner that would become commonplace. Photographer Alfred Wertheimer said the RCA room "looked like a set from a 1930's science fiction movie," different vectors of "monolithic half-cylinders" running along the acoustic tile, fluorescent lighting pipes up top, wood floors with a patch of carpet for the instruments. An utter remove. At one point, his drummer "laid Elvis' leather-covered guitar across his lap and played the back of it with a mallet, to get an additional snare effect." The goal? "When they finally got the sound that he was looking for, Elvis pronounced, "That felt good." He took a copy of "Hound Dog" on the long train ride back to Memphis, to learn what he'd recorded, playing it repeatedly, like a fan, on a portable device.[7]

Popular memory tags Presley's September debut on *The Ed Sullivan Show* as his 1956 epitome, but the program was a ~~minstrel~~ variety show jumble. Sullivan, recovering from a car accident, couldn't be there: the guest host, Charles Laughton, an English actor, quoted Keats poems alongside mildly ribald limericks. Musically, apart from Elvis, Dorothy Sarnoff from Broadway's *The King and I* offered an Orientalist fantasy; a quartet called the Vagabonds, with accordion, comic upright bass, and a guitarist who anticipated Chuck Berry's duckwalk goofed through Hoagy Carmichael's "Lazy River"; "I'm in the Mood for Love" was belted by "New Face of 1956" Amru Sani, presented as being from India (nobody now is quite sure). And "Hound Dog" wasn't the only dog: a cute pooch took commands from not-so-lovely Igor. Presley, too, couldn't be at the theater: he and the Jordanaires were filmed in Hollywood. A quick "Hound Dog" was introduced by Presley, his comportment fit for the Sullivan show's determined mix of anti-elitist gentility and relentless schtick: "As a great philosopher once said, 'You . . .'"[8]

In other ways, the *Sullivan* show did offer a coronation. Representing Elvis in the theater with Laughton were four gold records, singles that had each sold a million copies, faster, viewers were told, than anybody had managed before. The singles sat there on the wall, accruing interest, while every other element of the program winked and cackled. If you could compare these gold objects to anything, it might be the "Big M" Mercury car, with its "roadability" touted in ads throughout the hour. The records, the car, were objects, not objects in motion so much as objects of motion. And objects of emotion: the screaming "ladies," as Elvis called them, weren't pictured, but they were heard, as with no other performer that evening, and Presley incorporated them into his act—he could bank on them, too.

Ultimately, Presley performed live on the program in a way that—ever so briefly—matched "Hound Dog" on the record. "Ready. Set. Go man go," he jabbed, coming from a different entertainment category, a different ethos, after so much Orientalism, minstrelsy, aw-shucks blasé. For two minutes and two seconds, covering Little Richard's "Ready Teddy," he rocked. Bobbed, played guitar, hung it all out. "Ready, ready, ready to rock and roll." He wasn't alone now, singing to a damn basset, need not relate to sketch partners, to Berle and the starlet, to Allen's arch existentialism. He had his trio to one side; his singers and a piano pounder to the other; amplifier in between; and lyrics tight enough to double-time: "sweetie pie," "apple of my eye." "Ready!" Thirty seconds in, and he'd already invoked rock and roll twice, then put his hand to his ear to receive the screamers, too. The next, and best, verse is about the "flat top cats and the dungaree dolls," imagined "headed for the gym to the sock hop ball," courtesy of white Mississippi songwriter John Marascalco, in collaboration with Black Seattle producer Bumps Blackwell. "The cats are going wild / The music really sends me / I dig that crazy style." I can pause the clip. See Elvis throw himself back to urge on Moore's brief solo. How fast it must have seemed, there to begin a new school year. Kick off your shoes.

Unable to rewind, revved Elvis viewers had one option: play the singles over and over, like Presley with his demo on the train to Tennessee. Fixate on moments in the recording as we now can the TV performance. The "Hound Dog" that quickly concluded Presley's first *Sullivan* appearance, just a verse, chorus, and bow, was back to the good-humored tone of the Berle appearance. Whatever transmogrification of playback and payback had produced the studio classic was not replicable a few months later. In his second *Sullivan* appearance, in October, Presley called "Hound Dog," with another wink, "one of the saddest songs you've ever heard. It really tells a story, friends. Beautiful lyrics"—and paused for the expected chuckles. "It goes something like this." Elvis, delivering his best Steve Allen. False starts, arm waves, laughing at the screams that precede the rapture. His hips were wiggling again; the letters came streaming in again. But it was more self-conscious: he crossed his legs and held back his body to Scotty's soloing, showing he could turn his and your body on as he chose. No lingering bump and grind. Song over, Sullivan and Elvis shook hands, the host left, and the King announced a Thanksgiving picture release and return to Sullivan's show in January, concluding, "God bless."

"Hound Dog" had gone from singularity to ritual. On the 1968 "comeback" TV special, it joined a black-leather medley of 1950s hits, sandwiched between "Heartbreak Hotel" and "All Shook Up." Presley took off his guitar, got on his knees, interjected some "snooping around my door" from Big Mama Thornton's version. Footage in 1970 shows that he revived the joke intro: "Hound Dog" is a "tender ballad" you sing by getting right up into a girl's face. "You ain't!—it blows her hair straight back." The band revved up, and the post–rock revolution King let the few words roll up into baby blather. He put his fist in his mouth to emphasize the imbecility of it all. In 1977 he barely enunciated "Hound Dog," two minutes of musical fodder in a sequence whose goal seemed to be to get as many as possible scarves sweated on and tossed out to the massive crowd. The rhythm was a church revival rave-up, stirring the spirit, with Black women backup singers clapping onstage.[9]

In the language of Bob Dylan, via Greil Marcus, "Hound Dog" was now part of what you might mean if you imagined the King of Rock and Roll, Big Papa Presley, singing "I Threw It All Away." Alice Walker's short story "Nineteen Fifty-Five" made Presley's inability to know what he had achieved a "ball don't lie" blues truth—she imagined a singer, modeled on Elvis, forced to visit a singer modeled on Thornton: "I done sung that song seem like a million times this year, he said. I sung it on the Grand Ole Opry. I sung it on the Ed Sullivan show. . . . I've sung it and sung it, and I'm making forty thousand dollars a day offa it, and you know what, I don't have the faintest notion what that song means." Maureen Mahon can't help noting, "Presley's version of the song didn't make sense." Presley "could not, as a heterosexual man, sing about the same kind of dog as Thornton." The resulting lyrics were "nearly nonsensical."[10]

But another view is possible. "Hound Dog" stayed what it had always been for Elvis, literary-auteurist musicking on the twitchy edge of gibberish: rock and roll. His act and his calling. Back in his Sun days, in control of nothing save his ability to impress Sam Phillips in a small room in Memphis, Presley covered "Good Rockin' Tonight." Guralnick has Marion Keisker testifying, "The sessions would go on and on. Each record was sweated out. Sam showed patience beyond belief—in a personality that's not really given to patience."[11] Roy Brown's original had more of a swing feel, finger-snapping suave—his rockin' shoes more like bowling shoes. Wynonie Harris, intended by Brown to be the singer, gave it a star turn: blues in his voice as he told his sweetie to meet him in the alley, and his sax player to rock, oh rock. But for both men, the rocking included elder Brown, deacon Jones, stomping at the jubilee, Sweet Georgia Brown and Caledonia: everybody who got down in church and everybody on the R&B jukebox. With Elvis, the song's situation shifted. The focus was on his voice, timbre twisting and beat dancing in aural snapshots only a whole session could capture, electric guitar matching the giddy kid's satisfied impishness, and back to "Well, we're gonna rock." A breakdown, a manifesto: "We're gonna rock all our blues away." Not cure them or learn to live with them. Eliminate them and homestead what the eternal punk band, the Mekons, in their song

"Memphis, Egypt," called "that secret place where we all want to go." Rock and roll.

Rock and roll. Sure, Presley might have thrown something of that magic away by the 1970s, lost access to it, but he was hardly alone. We can hear rueful testimony in the lyrics of other big Elvis fans in the post-1960s rock world, aware that their childhood record collections had been not revived but eclipsed by the solidification of rock as taste, counterculture, and industry format, sometime between the Beatles photographed on the EMI stairwell the first time (Red Album cover) and the second time (Blue Album cover). Hard-drumming Led Zeppelin, "Rock and Roll": "Been a long time since I rock and rolled." Falsetto Elton John, "Crocodile Rock": "I remember when rock was young." These records, one made for arena use, the other a Top 40 manifesto, pushed to rerecord the previous era's now-estranged sounds, like codes to a lock, passages back to Narnia.

Rock and roll, secret place and unsustainable hallucination. It failed Big Mama Thornton, scorned Patti Page. And if "Hound Dog" is evidence, even Elvis Presley didn't feel fully at home there. The 1950s produced a jukebox's worth of songs whose recording process sealed all sorts of cultural complexity in the studio but represented a singularity, a category quandary, in the world outside. As with the vernacular singers caught fully in the mid-1920s, this was an eruption of voices from margins, but electrified amateurs cut off even from the patronizing context that "old-timey," "race records," and "down home" had earlier represented.

There's a funny echo in the popular-music literature that speaks to this refusal of collectivity and settled place. In both the early pages of Spörke's Thornton biography and the epigraph of Mahon's chapter on Thornton in *Black Diamond Queens*, you can read from an interview Big Mama did where she says the expected, "My singing comes from my experience"; notes her lack of formal training ("I taught myself to sing and to blow harmonica and even to play drums by watchin' other people"); and then concludes, "I can't read music but I know what I'm singing! I don't sing like nobody but myself."[12] Now Albin Zak's book, subtitled *Remaking Music in 1950s America*, has the title *I Don't Sound Like Nobody*—and it isn't due to Big Mama Thornton. The first Presley book, really a fan booklet, *Elvis Presley Speaks*!, published by the fan magazine *Rave* in 1956, had the singer telling Keisker during their first meeting at Sun, "I don't sing like nobody but me I reckon." That became "I don't sound like nobody" in the Jerry Hopkins 1971 biography, *Elvis*, where much in the legend solidified.[13]

Zak connects Patti Page, Big Mama Thornton, and Elvis Presley in the postwar recording studio. All participated in a moment where "reverb and capturing echoes distinguished records from acoustic reality." At Sun, Zak argues, "Phillips had steered the young singer and shown him the creative potential inherent in record making." By his first sessions for RCA Victor, at the beginning of 1956, which produced "Heartbreak Hotel," Presley "produced his own recordings"—a quote from engineer Bones Howe.

Presley's energy in the studio produced "a low-tech, raucous punch with mix balances featuring an aggressive vocal presence, a crackshot snare, pumping bass, and Scotty Moore's incisive electric guitar." He ignored standard session lengths: "No clocks, no boundaries." It wasn't professional: the Jordanaires came off "like an oblivious harmonium caught at the wrong recording date." English critic Steve Race called it "a thoroughly bad record." But *bad* meaning *good* is part of the US pop ABCs—as Zak writes, "Crudeness was not a matter of inferior resources or skill but a wholly intentional aesthetic choice" that "legitimized apparently amateur noise making." The song belonged to a "new sonic realm where the project was no longer capturing reality but creating it."[14]

Big Mama Thornton didn't sing like nobody: "Hound Dog" in the first version fed on that, in ways we have been expanding our awareness of these days, given how little recognition she received in her life. Elvis Presley didn't sing like nobody: "Hound Dog" in the second version made hay of that, too, in ways we have been revising ever since, necessary given how ridiculously much recognition he received initially. Both versions—and "Doggie" makes three—created a fixed unreality in the form of 1950s singles. Afterward, something in the grooves fought, largely in vain, to become a social fact.

# 05 "Hound Dog" as Influence

**THAT RCA LOGO OF NIPPER HEARING** "his master's voice" coming out of the speaker and thinking the dude was there might be claiming a bit much. Still, a recording transfers: you can take it places, far from the where, what, when, and why that produced it. Mark Katz delineates in *Capturing Sound* such qualities as tangibility, portability, (in)visibility, repeatability, temporality, receptivity, and manipulability. Alexander Weheliye's *Phonographies* finds correspondences between what W. E. B. Du Bois was up to in *Souls of Black Folks* and the quintessential DJ composition: the mix. That great literary listener, Ralph Ellison, writing in almost the same moment as this book's core songs, placed his *Invisible Man* in a basement, the better to hear Satchmo's piercing trumpet and vernacular wit:

> Now I have one radio-phonograph; I plan to have five. There is a certain acoustical deadness in my hole, and when I have music I

> want to feel its vibration, not only with my ear but with my whole body. I'd like to hear five recordings of Louis Armstrong playing and singing "What Did I Do to Be so Black and Blue"—all at the same time. Sometimes now I listen to Louis while I have my favorite dessert of vanilla ice cream and sloe gin. I pour the red liquid over the white mound, watching it glisten and the vapor rising as Louis bends that military instrument into a beam of sound. Perhaps I like Louis Armstrong because he's made poetry out of being invisible. I think it's because he's unaware that he is invisible. And my own grasp of invisibility aids me to understand his music.

The allure of recording and playback named the aficionado magazine *Hi Fidelity*, where in the 1950s columnist Roland Gelatt told the story in columns that became *The Fabulous Phonograph*: his chapter "Recording Becomes Electric," on the 1920s, preceded talk of "Dylan Goes Electric" by a full decade. Missing acoustically produced discs: now that's retro.[1]

Elvis Presley never played England—his manager, Colonel Parker, was undocumented, among other reasons. His records traveled there. Singles on the road, electrified and indivisible. In the memoir *Me*, Elton John recalled his mom bringing home a "Heartbreak Hotel" disc. He knew Elvis's name, had encountered "Rock Around the Clock," but "'Heartbreak Hotel' didn't sound anything like that either. It was raw and sparse and slow and eerie. . . . It didn't matter what he was saying, because something almost physical happened while he was singing. You could literally *feel* this strange energy he was giving off, like it was contagious. . . . As 'Heartbreak Hotel' played, it felt like something had changed, that nothing could really be the same again."[2] Keith Richards talked in *Life* about "Heartbreak" in similar terms.

> That was the first rock and roll I heard. It was a totally different way of delivering a song, a totally different sound, stripped down, burnt, no bullshit, no violins and ladies' choruses and schmaltz, totally different. It was bare, right to the roots that you had a feeling were there but hadn't yet heard. I've got to take my hat off to Elvis for that. The silence is your canvas, that's your frame, that's what you work on; don't try and deafen it out. That's what "Heartbreak Hotel" did to me. It was the first time I'd heard something so stark.[3]

Add to the choir John Lennon, who made clear in 1965, "Nothing really affected me until I heard Elvis. If there hadn't been an Elvis, there wouldn't have been the Beatles." Lennon told Jann Wenner, "There is nothing conceptually better than rock and roll. No group, be it Beatles, Dylan or Stones, have ever improved on 'Whole Lotta Shakin' Goin' On,' for my money. Or maybe I'm like our parents: That's my period, and I dig it and I'll never leave it." He added in 1975, "It was Elvis who really got me out of Liverpool." In one of his last interviews, he said, "When I was 16, Elvis was what was happening. A guy with long hair wiggling his ass and singing 'Hound Dog' and 'That's All Right,'"[4]

My goal is not to stack up boomer testimonials: we know "Elvis Presley Mattered," "John Lennon Mattered," all too well—I'm happy to await DJ Lynnée Denise's "Why Big Mama Thornton

Matters." But mark the insecurity in Lennon's account of his taste, his feeling that he might be left out of the rock format developed in the 1970s. In something of the same way critical taste of late has flipped from Presley to Thornton, the screamer and rock and roller Lennon, shredding his voice to represent raw artistry, has lost ground to Paul McCartney, repping musicianship and an enduring place in the industry. "Hound Dog" as transfixing oddity wasn't resolvable for those, like Lennon, who it most deeply affected. To use his friend Elton's metaphor, its impact proved contagious. As a problem, to cite Richards, "that's what you work on." Diagnosing what intensities like "Hound Dog" meant came to produce a text-around-text Talmudic impulse inside rock and roll discourse.

The angsty result was audible in one stop on the "Hound Dog" journey: Lennon, onstage at Madison Square Garden in 1972, singing it backed by the sax-driven Elephant's Memory. On the album *Live in New York City*, you can hear him going all in, relishing the repetition, the notes about class and lies—and, faintly, you can hear Yoko Ono making noise alongside; Lennon shouts love to Elvis to end it all. A video version makes Ono more prominent: the *arf arf*s of Patti Page, Big Mama Thornton, and Freddie Bell played for agitprop and camp.[5] There's 1950s dancing by the hippies onstage, like when Sha Na Na did "Hound Dog," a pounding piano, Lennon pumping his voice through a bullhorn. The most Dylanesque of Beatles had the most to work through about what rock and roll meant, and that labor always registered. His final press cycle included comments about Ono's formative relationship to postpunk and new wave. Ono had gotten something on record not heard before; it was a story Lennon was amply prepared to register.

Bruce Springsteen, an American apostle of "Hound Dog," opted to twist and shout to sort the "Hound Dog" questions all out, the pope of rock and roll's Catholic Reformation. He leaned on Clarence Clemons on the *Born to Run* album cover, with an Elvis the King button pinned to his black leather jacket. Springsteen as rocker connected the garage-band singles aesthetic that became New York punk, the Dylan notion of going electric to amplify folksinger messages, and the Stones and Zep arena model. The Boss became a dad whose kid pursued competitive show horse riding. High class. But it was not a lie when he would show up at the Stone Pony on the Jersey Shore—there's audio footage on YouTube of him covering "Hound Dog" there with the house band, and if I'm not mistaken, it's the Little Richard version of the song, from *Don't Knock the Rock*, that he's alluding to with the opening intro. Positively curatorial.[6]

Springsteen delivered the South By Southwest convention keynote in 2012, underlining his whiteness as he once had his sax player's Blackness: "In the beginning, every musician has their genesis moment. For you, it might have been the Sex Pistols, or Madonna, or Public Enemy. It's whatever initially inspires you to action. Mine was 1956, Elvis on the *Ed Sullivan Show*. It was the evening I realized a white man could make magic, that you did not have to be constrained by your upbringing, by the way you looked, or by the social context that oppressed you. You could call upon your own powers of imagination, and you could create a transformative self." The Boss would take this show into a memoir, *Born to Run*, and a Broadway performance, too. Presley on Sullivan's show was the big bang, presented in the book with all-caps semisarcasm as "THE BARRICADES HAVE BEEN STORMED!! A FREEDOM SONG HAS BEEN SUNG!!" In smaller notes, Springsteen matched Elvis to his own medicated, psychoanalyzed, inauthentic twenty-first-century performing self: "He was a showman, an entertainer, an imaginer of worlds, an unbelievable success, an embarrassing failure and a fount of modern action and ideas." And as he told BBC Radio 4 in explaining why "Hound Dog" was one of his eight desert-island discs, "We still base our snare drum sound, one of the ultimate snare drum sounds, on Hound Dog."[7]

Neil Young found other ways to rub his stick against what "Hound Dog" had done. Blowing up *Saturday Night Live* in 1989, with a performance of "Rockin' in the Free World," the key line "Don't feel like Satan but I am to them," he wore an Elvis T-shirt, the same mixture of punk and classic rock he'd centered in "it's better to burn out than fade away" around when he put Sex Pistols short-circuit up against Graceland moldiness: "The king is gone but he's not forgotten / This is the story of Johnny Rotten." I've always been fond of "Old King," from the 1992 *Harvest Moon*, about Young's dog, so to speak: "Old King sure meant a lot to me /

But that hound dog is history." He'd come back to the topic with *Prairie Wind*'s "He Was the King"—Elvis shooting televisions, singing gospel, a Vegas dream, a three-piece band, the silver screen. "And the whole world sang along." Young's hatred of compact discs and MP3s, love of sounds he could make with his guitar Old Black or his band of fuck-ups, Crazy Horse, was "Hound Dog," too—efforts at electric alchemy. His 1990s included a Crazy Horse tour with Sonic Youth opening so the sound could magnify, an album reflecting on Kurt Cobain's suicide note about not fading away, a Pearl Jam collaboration inspiring one final effort to catch the rabbit: "I'm the Ocean."

By the late 1980s, when induction into the Hall of Fame replaced induction into the army as a central element of the rock narrative, Elvis was still, to quote indie rocker Mojo Nixon, everywhere. Everything. Still the King. Chuck D of Public Enemy said Elvis didn't mean shit to him, but what Public Enemy tried to do, bringing the noise, remained wed to the notion of the studio producing the secret place we all want to go. You could hear the Sun Records reverb in even the group's failed first album; Run-D.M.C. with "Rock Box" and "Kings of Rock" had claimed the throne and PE wanted to live in Run's house. Eddie Murphy kept an Elvis shrine and lived in his own version of Graceland once Hollywood checks came in. Bob Dylan told *Us* magazine, in 1987, "When I first heard Elvis' voice I just knew that I wasn't going to work for anybody; and nobody was going to be my boss. He is the deity supreme of rock and roll religion as it exists in today's form. Hearing him for the first time was like busting out of jail."[8]

Bruno Mars was all but born into this reality: at age six, in a jumpsuit, with a pompadour, he was already on *The Arsenio Hall Show* in 1991 singing "Heartbreak Hotel," making trembles instead of rumbles but fully committed to the shake. Hall gave him a week of groceries as a prize. In the 1990 documentary *Viva Elvis*, Mars, just four, sneered in profile, called "tomorrow's king of rock and roll." Interviewed, he said, "I like his singing and his dancing and his lips." What Elvis songs did he know? "I know 'Trouble' and 'Blue Suede Shoes' and 'Hound Dog.'" Cut to him pumping his waist to "you ain't never caught a rabbit and . . ." His uncle explained that Bruno grew up in his Elvis memorabilia store, modeled on the one near Graceland, handling the merchandise, saturated in the image.[9]

Americanization, British Invasion, sacralization, postmodernity: old "Hound Dog" participated in all of these, without ever becoming less inherently strange. Still, if you were Eric Clapton on the 1989 *Journeyman* album (critic Robert Christgau: "What did you expect him to call it—*Hack*?"), you covered the Thornton version of "Hound Dog," which had its own trajectory, one that returned the song to Blackness and white "blackness."[10] Just as Thornton came up as a new Bessie Smith, Koko Taylor and Etta James in their versions were new Big Mamas. Taylor did it on the 1993 album *Force of Nature* as Alligator Records electric blues for brewpubs—Buddy Guy backed her on a different number, as he once had Thornton. James covered the song on the 2000 *Matriarch of the Blues* as rolling New Orleans funk, with affectionate *arfs* as she sang to the accompaniment of family members and Meters guitarist Leo Nocentelli. James Taylor tried to join the party remotely in his 2008 *Covers* version, placed after Leonard Cohen's "Suzanne" with Yo-Yo Ma on cello—grown-up music about life's pleasures from a barn in Massachusetts. There was nothing epistemological to reconcile about performing the Thornton "Hound Dog," no chain to jerk. To recall Maureen Mahon's opposing view of Presley's take, this "Hound Dog" made sense.

Another way to locate the difference is that the Big Mama "Hound Dog" belonged to the long tradition of groove music, where the individual performer connected to the community like a call-and-response. Thornton herself could be seen, worn and near death, singing "Hound Dog" in the 1984 documentary *Legends of Rhythm and Blues*, part of an educational series called *Repercussions: A Celebration of African-Influenced Music.*[11] She sat for most of the performance, winking and smoking to stay mobile and engaged, but at the very end of "Hound Dog," she danced, as best she could, as she had always done when the band played it to her beat. In some performances she'd throw in the name of a current dance craze, as James Brown did. Presley's version of "Hound Dog" had a live-TV history, then a studio encapsulation—an identity crisis waiting to happen. Thornton's "Hound Dog" kept inviting new dogs to the festivities. The "bow wow wow" riffs that

Koko Taylor put in her version evoked George Clinton's "Atomic Dog," already repurposed in Black pop as Snoop Dogg's "Who Am I (What's My Name)?"

Rapper DMX's "Get At Me Dog" entered the pantheon not long afterward. Many things about DMX were tortured and complicated: his upbringing, his drug use, his view of sin and salvation. But as a reporter who once sat in a small office with X and his pit bulls, attempting an interview, I can attest that his identification with his dogs—their playing, barking, biting, loving—was fully aligned with his music and his persona. Using the song to launch a set of chart-topping albums, DMX took on rock-star qualities, as Snoop had: the individual rebel artist who could be loved by daydreaming teen boys of all races. As with Thornton in her day, X's physical presence seemed to portend a storming of the cultural gates. And, also like Thornton, his personal life, easy to project onto his growl and forcefulness, masked a literary quality—each act of DMXpression arrived with the cadence of stage verse. On record, we were pushed to hear X as part of a collective crew, the Ruff Ryders. Profiling him, tales of mugging people—even this a kind of social relationship, the way he told it—intersected with hip-hop memories of a club battle with Jay-Z. At one point in the *GQ* feature process, he drove me through Harlem, blaring his own music, to make kids look up and rush his way when he paused at stoplights. "Get At Me Dog" belonged to a nation under a groove, even if this neoliberal era Dog wasn't the Atomic Dog.

"Hound Dog" by Presley traveled as a recording to warp ears and minds; "Hound Dog" by Thornton offered what Amiri Baraka might have called a "changing same" groove. Can we hear iterations and extensions of the dreaded "Doggie in the Window," too? Not many. Freddy Fender's take made the song's gender dynamics more conventional but added a Spanish-language second half. A UK hit recording competed with Page's, by Liverpool's Lita Roza, which Roza hated and Margaret Thatcher declared her favorite record of all time. Thin stuff. But what if we brought in that notable dog lover, Laurie Anderson? Gayle Wald calls this "Listening to the B-Side of History," the cultural imaginaries that obscurities can summon for us.[12] "Hound Dog" has a paucity of B-sides: "Nightmare," another Jerry Leiber and Mike Stoller number, far more torchy and vibes-driven in the case of Thornton; "Don't Be Cruel," such a big hit on its own terms that Presley's single was called a double-A record—kings don't live on the B-side of history. "Doggie" had as its B-side "My Jealous Eyes," lyrics by Hal David's older brother, Mack, and ballroom Latin rhythms by Martita, the writing name of Margery Cummings, who would help connect Hal with Burt Bacharach on the three's later cowrite "Tell the Truth and Shame the Devil."

Anderson was fated to walk on the B-side. A performance artist who defined that category with a mixture of post–John Cage musical approaches (treated violin rather than piano) and shaggy-dog storytelling, she manipulated her vocals to range from "voice of authority" masculinity to multiplicity and flatness, adding an unexpected tenderness that turned posthuman scenarios into sentimental landscapes. On her first single, the unlikely 1981 number-two British pop hit "O Superman," she was the postmodern version of multitracking Patti Page. Where the Patti Page of "Doggie in the Window" offered furry fluff soon to be crunched to slobberbones by the vernacular, Anderson made arty pop as an avatar of what Fred Moten would title, for the first big section of *In the Break*, "the sentimental avant-garde."[13] Everything dismissible about Page, Anderson weaponized.

And this shifting of provocation points became the subject of the "O Superman" B-side, a great one, called "Walk the Dog." Same tools: voice manipulation and minimalism played for cabaret, sensibility all New York. One can walk the dog in billiards, with a yo-yo; the Rufus Thomas hit of that name has a pattern so ingrained in other musical patterns that it reifies groove, akin to the trees made entirely of wood in Anderson's song, the dog thirty feet high, on a movie screen, made entirely of light, the wonderful party with interesting people made entirely of *mm-hmms*. Anderson only gets specific on one verse:

> *I turned on the radio and I heard a song by Dolly Parton.*
> *And she was singing:*
> *Oh! I feel so sad! I feel so bad!*
> *I left my mom and I left my dad.*
> *And I just want to go home now.*
> *I just want to go back in my Tennessee mountain home now.*

*Well, you know she's not gonna go back home.*
*And I know she's not gonna go back home.*
*And she knows she's never gonna go back there.*
*And I just want to know who's gonna go and walk her dog.*

She called this eradication—of Roland Barthes's "grain of the voice" in wood, pets, Parton, and Manhattan dinner theater—her country and western song on *Late Night with David Letterman*, whose host seemed irked that she was going after the beloved Dolly. But her target could as easily have been Elvis—in an appearance with life partner Lou Reed on *Charlie Rose*, she says, "I could see through that" about a Lou courting maneuver, and it's game-set-match.[14]

Anderson in 2022 delivered several intoxicating multimedia online Norton Lectures. In the first, "The River," she recalled the first 45 she owned, given her by a relative when she was four or five, called "Letters from Daddy." The voice of a man reading notes to his daughter. "And once in a while there were explosions. So there was obviously a war going on. And there were lots of long pauses, like he was looking out over the edge of the trench, or like I was supposed to be saying things to him, also. And it was the first time I realized that records were a collaboration between the performer and the listener, both of them getting lost in the sound."[15]

The chance to get lost in sound, or, better, found in it, is what records offer. That's the paradigm here, the dynamic that as

"Hound Dog" and "Doggie" played out didn't turn out to mean the unquestionable triumph of rock and roll but also wouldn't fully accommodate a revision built on clear intersections of race, class, gender, sexuality, and region. Matters were all just too slippery. How might an artist successfully let literary or auteurist musicking perform that uncertainty? What Page offered, compressed as a snow globe, to the considerable irritation of listeners who wanted to believe in Black music or rock and roll, Anderson writ large. In conceptual performance she made vocality questions into a story. And as the vernacular revolution became suspect, that way of voicing the slippages—*not* trying to sound like nobody else, distant from the whole competition—registered powerfully.

More true confessions: I wrote bitterly about Americana singer Gillian Welch's "reverence" for old music when she debuted, in my short-lived *Spin* "Whatever" column. (Hey, it was peak alt-rock.) Instead, I recommended Nick Tosches on lost blackface minstrel Emmett Miller and got a thank-you note from the chronicler of hellfire and twisted roots. But many consider "Elvis Presley Blues" by Welch a few years later the great musical rumination on the dying King. To an acoustic guitar pattern that might trace to early recording maestro Mississippi John Hurt, Welch contemplates the country boy who rocked and the rockers who heard him as "like a hurricane," "like a midnight rambler," then left him alone for "the long decline." The tale is not resolved: the only referenced Elvis song is "All Shook Up." But the tone is statement enough. Stop looking for the next mystery train to jump out from the stereo, it patiently insists. Welch's delivery lives outside Page, Thornton, and Presley. She's a lapsed believer, regretful about any part she may have played in the rock and roll corn harvest. I should have listened softer.

# 06 Interpreting "Hound Dog"

**AS I SUSPECT YOU KNOW,** a lot of books have been written about Elvis Presley. Here I have a particular genealogy to trace. How did writers over time find language for "Hound Dog" the single, for rock and roll the craze, for the confusing works of magnetically recorded magnetism plus intersectional identity that prefigured the social movements needed to unpack them?

Start with the music writers, already adults, who heard "Hound Dog" in 1955 as jazz and blues fans. Rudi Blesh, the trad jazz and ragtime collector tied to bohemian art scenes, wrote in a revision of his *Shining Trumpets*, "The 'funky boys' are not playing it safe. They want to play hot with deep, unabashed feeling; they want to rock and wail." Samuel Charters, popularizer of *Country Blues* in 1959, in 1992 published a novel called *Elvis Presley Calls His Mother after the Ed Sullivan Show*, shrewd on media back in the 1950s, on women fans and southern parents—a book of unresolved urges from Robert Browning on the goat god Pan to Elvis perishing of incomprehension. If Laurie Anderson recalled letters from a dad to a daughter, here is the imagined voice of a son to a mother.

> "Now Momma, you got to understand I didn't have no idea what all those camera people were doing when the show went out over the air. I know Mr. Sullivan had some kind of idea to make people sit up a little by having just the top part of me showing on the screen, but I couldn't tell anything different was happening when I was doing my show. Is that what they did? You couldn't see what I was doing with my legs? You couldn't see anything at all below where I have my guitar hanging when I go out there on stage? I know what you're telling me, but I can't hardly believe that. I think some of the girls that were watching at home, I think those girls are feeling they missed the best part."

There were challenges for this cohort of writers, to whom we could add former swing kid Robert Johnson (a different one), reporting from Memphis in *Elvis Presley Speaks!*, and Harlan Ellison, pulp fiction author and former barracks mate of singer Buddy Knox, in the 1961 novel *Rockabilly*, aka *Spider Kiss*. One was to accept as valid the shifts in taste that went with substituting rock and roll for jazz values. The other, related, was to not see the shift as a mass cultural pseudo-event.[1]

For the white jazz gap, consider a movie version of Elvis Presley storming out of a party. In the 1957 *Jailhouse Rock*, his character, Vince Everett, a construction worker just out of jail and pursuing a music career, goes with a promoter who's helping him to a shindig at her parents' house. Dad is a professor, and the banter strains at hip: Dave Brubeck, progressive jazz, atonality, Dixieland. Everything in this scene speaks to class and region. Vince is offered bourbon and asks for beer. His southern accent stands out in contrast to the toniness of diction. Presley receives a jazz police–type question more condescending than anything that the previous year's Bing Crosby and Frank Sinatra vehicle *High Society* aimed at Louis Armstrong. Pompadour and sneer equally cocked and loaded, he delivers his line, "Lady, I don't know what the hell you talking about," and leaves the building.

For what I mean by pseudo-event, read Albert Goldman, who would try to kill, for posterity, both Presley and John Lennon but seemed to genuinely love Lenny Bruce. One expects, reading his Elvis book, to find dismissals like the view that Presley's "notion of what was hip was almost quaint." But not necessarily these subtle comparisons: "The important thing is to recognize that the root of rock is the put-on and the take-off, the characteristic fusion of enthusiasm and mockery that was almost universal in the pop culture of the fifties: a slant on things that you find as much in *Mad* or the routines of Sid Caesar or the comic pornography of Terry Southern as you do in the funny songs of Leiber and Stoller or the funny singing of Elvis Presley." Goldman: theorist of literary-auteurist musicking? In that role, he allowed a few vocalized hiccups as part of a pantheon he turned out to share with his greatest detractor, Greil Marcus: Elvis's Sun Records "might even be considered the comic flip side to the even denser and more suggestive blues fantasias of that other brilliant young recording genius, Robert Johnson." Ultimately, though, the sell-out was all that mattered, for Goldman ("the art is done for the money and the money is the measure of the art") no less than Institute of Jazz Studies founder Marshall Stearns, who called Presley "a tasteless version of the real thing."[2]

Commercialism and jazz were not worries for the next cohort of authors, figures like the young 1960s flamethrower Nik Cohn, child of "Hound Dog" and its mysteries, who simply wrote, "Elvis is where pop begins and ends" in a book whose title was *Pop from the Beginning* in the United Kingdom, *Rock from the Beginning* in the United States, and, finally, *Awopbopaloobop Awopbamboom* everywhere. To Cohn, the teen targeting of pop defined its power: that Little Richard bleat from "Tutti Frutti," like "Hound Dog," was the studio sealing in not only a moment of sound but the time in life granted for endless summer. Could pop grow up? "I'm not sure there's any real answer." In *Rock Dreams*, a book of paintings by Belgian Guy Peellaert of the pop-rock mythos from afar, Cohn's accompanying text concluded, "All you do is daydream. These daydreams, more than anything, are what this book is about. Rock as a secret society, as an enclosed teen fantasy."[3]

Back in the United States, three rock critics defined Elvis in different influential ways. Stanley Booth was the southerner who could write for invading Brits, touring America with the Rolling Stones in 1969 and stopping in Muscle Shoals with them to record "Brown Sugar." Nobody better mapped the world Presley might have seen had he left Graceland and Vegas more often, a spectrum from blues Furry Lewis to Beat William S. Burroughs. Booth claimed his feature on Presley's 1960s decline, "A Hound Dog to the Manor Born," helped prod the comeback special. In another article, "Fascinating Changes," he said to Fred Ford, "I can't believe I'm sittin' next to the man who barked like a dog at the end of Big Mama Thornton's 'Hound Dog.'" Ford replied, "I was gonna meow like a cat, but it was too hip for 'em."[4]

Peter Guralnick came south to collect lore, deposited in chapters of *Feel Like Going Home* and *Lost Highway* and in the entry on Elvis Presley in the *Rolling Stone Illustrated History of Rock & Roll*. Guralnick would become more ecumenical when he wrote Presley's biography, learning from women who identified as much with the ballads as the rockers. But his 1970s work championed the Sun Records Elvis, pieced together after the fact by boomer kids operating without trustworthy compilations, valuing the man from Tupelo who got real real gone. This was, as Guralnick pointed out in his *Rolling Stone Illustrated History* entry, work done in the face of ridicule: to Woodstock boomers the movie star Elvis was high fructose. Even so, the terms of the redemption Guralnick offered—to put Presley in a pantheon with blues and country singers, name him the greatest of those in-betweeners from whom followed figures like Charlie Rich—concealed no small contempt for the Elvis most fans loved. Greil Marcus called Guralnick's take on later Presley as the Sun work setting a "narrow vision" because "there is no greater aesthetic thrill than to see minority culture aggressively and triumphantly transform itself into mass culture."[5]

Yet it was also Marcus who wrote, "I think the real intent of Warhol's *Elvises* was to make you doubt that Elvis Presley ever did have that power, that he was ever an artist." That take thirty-one spirit of "Hound Dog" informed Marcus's approach: his book on the single "Like a Rolling Stone" went version by version through Dylan's recording process, concluding that what they finally played back wasn't what anybody had expected or could re-create. When I was ordering my entries in *Songbooks*, a survey of music books by publication year, I loved that Marcus's *Mystery Train* would be followed by *Resistance through Rituals*, the founding statement of Birmingham cultural studies coedited by Stuart Hall. But the split that represented, from rock criticism investing the popular with revolutionary possibility to dialectical, not to mention academic, conjunctural mappings, concealed a unity—the need to challenge, in the name of ordinary people, what historian E. P. Thompson famously set down as "the enormous condescension of posterity."[6]

"Hound Dog" turns up nine times in the index to *Mystery Train*, as the first Elvis that Marcus owned (bringing home the unnerving thrill), as a taste-ranking against the postcomeback Memphis stuff that was "not one I ever want to make," as work by an artist who "strolled into the studio and didn't leave until every note was perfect." Marcus started with the notion that, from his perch in the 1950s, not worried like Hank Williams or questioned by Black Power, Presley "had no guilty dues to pay." (Rocking all blues away.) He declared that Elvis sang "That's All Right" "with more power, verve, and skill" than its Black originator, Arthur "Big Boy" Crudup. True, he noted, Crudup and Thornton claimed "that Elvis would have been nothing without them, that he climbed to fame on their backs." To which he emptied a cartridge: "It is probably time to say that this is nonsense; the mysteries of black and white in American music are just not that simple. Consider the tale of 'Hound Dog.' "[7]

And so he did, from Jerry Leiber and Mike Stoller, then Presley, as the whites who wrote it and popularized it, to its status as a " 'black' song, unthinkable outside the impulses of black music." This led to one of those shrugs you now make with an emoticon: "Can you pull justice out of *that* mess?" We have already moved past the taste-ranking that Marcus very much did want to supply, that "Elvis heard the record, changed the song completely, from the tempo to the words, and cut Thornton's version to shreds." Marcus's conclusion anticipated the language of *American Idol* judges in the 2000s (or, my unmoved editor Joshua Clover notes, the argument of Manifest Destiny): "This was Elvis's music because he made it his own." Then it was on to "Louie Louie" as an even better story of amalgamation. In the "Notes and Discographies" section of the book, updated for constant new editions, Marcus returned to "Hound Dog," noting new charges of appropriation by Alice Walker and others. Not as aggressively confronting them this time, he deflected with the story of Leiber in an interracial communist commune, being lambasted the night "Hound Dog" was recorded "on why our excitement had no real social value." Another staple in the notes became an account of a 1957 concert in Seattle, where the King asked the crowd to rise for the national anthem—"You ain't . . ."—and that crowd included a school-age Jimi Hendrix.[8]

In the next round of scrutiny, critics mingled but no longer dominated, and Elvis was as much velvet curio and American flag as artist. Don DeLillo's novel *White Noise* posited Elvis studies as quintessential postmodern goop. (DeLillo, based on the earlier *Great Jones Street*, was more of a Dylan guy.) Gilbert Rodman's *Elvis after Elvis* registered the King in exactly these cultural studies terms—parading signifiers and signifieds. Women were heard from as authors on Presley, far more than with the Beatles or Dylan, emphasizing southern lineages, romance, and portions of Presley's life as far from "Hound Dog" as possible. When Guralnick wrote his great opening biography volume on the singer's "rise," he made this more expanded take into what Dylan called, in a blurb for it, a book that "cancels out the others." Marcus, Guralnick, Dylan—we might want to mention a presidential candidate from Arkansas, appearing on *The Arsenio Hall Show* in 1992 to play, however badly, "Heartbreak Hotel" on saxophone. Marcus responded with a book, *Double Trouble*, on Bill Clinton and Presley combined—the only way out of Reagan–Bush, it seemed then.[9] This stretch of writing overlapped the years between punk and grunge; boomers as deflating counterculture morphed into boomers as a new string of presidents.

Then something happened: Elvis Presley's iconicity cracked into human-sized pieces, and writing about him calmed down considerably. "Yabba Dabba Doo," George Jones had sung in 1989, "The King Is Gone (So Are You)," as the Berlin Wall fell and Cold War rock and roll verities began to splinter. "The "Elvis Is Everywhere" vantage of Mojo Nixon and Skid Roper in 1987 didn't disappear, but it got particularized. These days, Nixon keeps his Mojo howling like a dog as a DJ on SiriusXM's Outlaw Country station, whose promos call him "the loon in the afternoon." That seems about right.

Academics registered the new, less heated environment as an opportunity to try some non-postmodern Elvis studies. In 1996 Robert Fink wandered into a gathering of English-department types talking rock, part of a major academic reconciliation with popular music. Fink determined to show why "new musicology" that didn't put the composer's notated text above all deserved a place at this table. He dug in with the help of a different "Elvis Everywhere," a Michael Daugherty piece for the Kronos Quartet mixing Presley impersonators with screechy string quartet effects Laurie Anderson fans might recognize. Fink started with a question for his departmental fellows—"Can you do Elvis?" He could, through a twist or two. Glenn Branca guitar symphonies putting the avant-garde outside classical record bins. "Candle in the Wind" as Princess Diana's mourning music, not symphonic pomp. Classical music motifs in hip-hop and soul—Beck sampling Schubert. Tape loops from Stockhausen to Chemical Brothers. How, Fink asked, could one "answer Susan Sontag's demand for a descriptive vocabulary of form that can give insight into the new sensibility—in particular, into the way popular music works materially to 'program sensations'"? To answer, he closed with the Presley "Hound Dog" as whiteness: "enforcing a strict rhythmic hierarchy by making an entire phrase of weak upbeats lead inexorably to a heavily stressed downbeat." Dropped the mic.[10]

Edward Comentale deposited Elvis revisionism inside a book whose introduction positioned him as a Gen X answer to Marcus, his *Sweet Air* a *Mystery Train* with room for Billy Joel fans from suburbia as much as old, weird Americans. *Sweet Air* saw the recording studio as a place of vernacular modernism, abstraction from reality: Charley Patton as modernist blues, Woody Guthrie talking blues as proto-counterculture. For Elvis, Comentale emphasized how "convulsive performances—all tics and spasms, jerky poses and juxtaposed styles—express neither the authenticity of region nor the immediacy of race, but the giddy mediation of all identity in the modern era. In other words, when it came to Elvis culture, repetition precedes renewal, and self-estrangement implies self-renewal." Comentale preferred the commodified, "sluttish" Presley. And Sun Records offered "the readymade production of sonic pleasure as the basis of a new fan culture." Slapback echo and "the way each noise—each abstract riff, shout, drum kick—threatened to derail the entire song." Rock and roll "resounded in the utopian realm of the self-contained studio." Why did "Hound Dog" make senseless sense? Because "That's All Right" had long since shown how song could be freed "from any expressive need or purpose, giving it over to the play of chance and the slutty activity of the drives."[11]

Adding history to the music and English disciplinarians, Michael Bertrand's *Race, Rock, and Elvis* focused on the white southerners who advocated for Presley in the years preceding 1960s civil rights. They helped integrate concerts and went through a sequence of history we are still coming to understand: the first accounts were so thoroughly centered on white boomers in northern places receiving rock and roll on their transistor radios that few even thought about white kids in Alabama or North Carolina. Bertrand debunked the invented story that Presley had said, "The only thing a Black man can do for me is buy my records and shine my shoes." Media myths, positive and negative, had dispelled specific lived experience—more proof of how difficult it was for unities in a recording studio to remix social norms.[12]

Each of these efforts—Fink, Comentale, Bertrand, and Albin Zak on 1950s recording styles—became a study in rock and roll as whiteness, twitching and agitating but not freeing the world. In the genealogy I am tracing here, these most recent glimpses of Elvis and "Hound Dog" arc back down from ballyhoo to Charters and the preboomer authors sensing in Presley as much a reduction from what swing jazz as integrated American pop offered as an expansion. The next wave of academic treatments returned Presley to sender altogether and saluted only Big Mama Thornton. Yabba dabba doo. We are more likely, at this moment, to notice work on white rock and roll when it comes from filmmakers, like Baz Luhrmann with *Elvis* or Ethan Coen with his 2022 documentary, *Jerry Lee Lewis: Trouble in Mind*, constructed around the 1950s and 1960s video clips that flew by the first time around but can now be returned to, fetishized, absorbed in full in the manner that records used to be. Seen and not just heard as auteurist musicking.

Elvis writing began with what amounted to side-eyes from jazz critics and pulp culture pioneers. Turned into a rock critical insistence on coherence that echoed the finality of singles, with chart placements transported from Joel Whitburn Top 40 books stamped on each *Rolling Stone Illustrated History* entry. Became an American pastime circa the rise of Clintons not named George. And now we have this gulf, between popular music studies folks of one stripe, giving us the warped nuances of how 1950s records rewrote reality and popular music studies, and folks of another, bringing race and gender realities home to stay. Unlike sainted punk Lester Bangs, I guarantee you nothing, but we may never disagree on anything again the way we have disagreed on Elvis.

▶ 07

# The Whiteness of the Wail

**I WAS PROUD OF THIS** Moby Dick of a chapter title when I sent the Singles series coeditors a book pitch, only to realize when proofing *Songbooks* that I'd nicked it. Gary Giddins's "The Whiteness of the Wail" appeared in a 1977 *Village Voice* issue, then in his first collection, *Riding on a Blue Note*. Giddins talked about saxophonist Art Pepper and the notion that the best white jazz musicians "chose a black aesthetic as the best possible source for self-examination." This was, Giddins wrote, "the only quality no black jazzman can offer . . . a personal search fraught with peril." Pepper's wail turned on "the cry in his music . . . the gift of swinging with melancholy that the best white jazz musicians have offered." Josh Kun beat me, too, his *Audiotopia* examining "the Jewishness of the wail" in Mickey Katz's parody jazz as a refusal of assimilation into whiteness.[1]

In my case, the white wail I meant was Elvis Presley in the recorded version of "Hound Dog" but even more the scream Iggy Pop used to kick off "T.V. Eye" on the 1970 Stooges album *Funhouse*. Several seconds' worth of expunging, expungement, expungesis, then finally guitar and rhythm section kicking in just where you would want them to. To find testimony to the joy of this, call up the *Almost Famous* scene featuring Philip Seymour Hoffman as Lester Bangs, appearing on early rock radio to discourse on music as "a place apart from the vast, benign lap of America." Hoff-Bangs flips through records, then "Iggy Pop! Amen!" and he's getting down to "Search and Destroy." Since this book favors canines, let's switch to a different Stooges recording, their anthem and debut single: "I Wanna Be Your Dog."

John Cale, recently split from the Velvet Underground, produced. There were three guitar chords, a piano note Cale rammed, and sleigh bells. Rate Your Music offers as descriptors "sexual, energetic, male vocals, raw, aggressive, rebellious, nihilistic, noisy, psychedelic, hedonistic, heavy, repetitive, anxious, apathetic." Listening, I notice how the opening is a theatrical and ritualistic setup. Then that guitar-bass-drum combination, modal and primal as Black Sabbath, putting you in the pit. Iggy sings only one-syllable words at first, making "Wanna," the bridging of two such, almost verbose; the Ramones would perfect this, and Bo Diddley predated it, but "I Wanna Be Your Dog" set the punk minimalism blueprint. From there, one could only augment: he sings "lose my heart in the burning sand." A mono version on YouTube has as web art a photo of the Elektra LP inserted inside the empty hole of the original 45, the borders a touch melted, psychedelic style.[2]

"I Wanna Be Your Dog" is a fitting end for the Elvis "Hound Dog" story because punk on its way to indie and alt-rock largely concluded rock and roll's white legacy of compacted recordings as willful singularities, sonic reducers. This wasn't the self-examination that Giddins found in jazz. Punks engaged in a different inquiry, the debate over what in post–hippie rock to negate. They exaggerated rock and roll archetypes to hear what a monster version might reveal. The studio void as backdrop, the single as schizophonic platform, and the serrated scream were all essential once again.

The resulting vinyl, though, operated differently in the world. Semipopular pop, in contrast to the omnipresent but socially unmoored "Hound Dog," produced cultural capital. This then became social capital as, in a decades-long process, scene and subculture became a hip, then a gentrifying, then an unaffordable neighborhood. Iggy Pop says his identity as Iggy came clear once his first record came out: in the classic fashion of Presley studying his own work product on the train back to Memphis, what made sense in the vinyl became something he had to interpret. But he also notes that his upbringing in collegiate Ann Arbor meant what he did in the Stooges wasn't so far from the "screaming sounds through amplifiers" of an avant-gardist like Robert

Ashley. Stooges punk helped produce a club on the Bowery. In time, that club became a John Varvatos boutique near a Whole Foods even as a grants-worthy version of the scene moved boroughs to the Brooklyn Academy of Music.[3]

"Be Your Dog" grew in stature over the years, a kind of increasingly orthodox summation statement. Sonic Youth made it a regular encore, performing it on the blink-and-you-missed-it TV show *Night Music* in 1989, the same year a still-new Nirvana recorded a sort-of cover with different words but the same vibe—apparently, if one follows the attributed link, that's also Nirvana doing it at Roseland as full-on stars in 1993, but with Jad Fair of Half-Japanese singing alongside British rock critic Everett True. The great TV show *Reservation Dogs* began its pilot episode with rez kids in an Oklahoma far from Patti Page's heisting a truck to its sonic potholes. R.E.M. covered the song alongside Patti Smith and her guitarist Lenny Kaye in the year they were all inducted into the Rock and Roll Hall of Fame, making "I Wanna Be Your Dog" the look-back-with-a-smile equivalent of what in earlier ceremonies might have been a Chuck Berry or Beatles song, a "Summertime Blues."[4]

What did it mean for Michael Stipe to wrap his arm around his inspiration, Smith, and sing, "So messed up I want you here . . . tonight I wanna be your dog . . . come on!"? (She sang the line about burning sand.) One clue came during R.E.M.'s acceptance, when Stipe noted that the band's main ambition when they formed was to play New York. You can read much about this in Grace Hale's history *Cool Town*, on their Athens, Georgia, scene, an exchange of southern style and downtown ratification from the B-52s' forward, queer, and punk identity mixed with pop ambition and indie sustainability. In the rock history I participated in as a college DJ, then itemized for the *Spin Alternative Record Guide* I edited after Nirvana broke, the pilgrimage gaining momentum from *Village Voice*-CBGB to University of Georgia college town to Minneapolis, Seattle, and beyond was as mesmerizing as the journey from Tupelo to *Ed Sullivan*. We made vague waves at race, gender, and class analysis, hadn't heard of neoliberalism yet or contemplated Sub Pop's relationship to Microsoft, Starbucks, and Amazon.[5]

Ryan Moore's *Sells Like Teen Spirit* connects those dots, but, as always, I want to think about singles and the legacy of "Hound Dog." Unlike Patti Page, Patti Smith was a rock and roller—it's fully there in the versioning of the quintessential rock song "Hey Joe" that she made the A side of her first single. "Hey Joe" had gone from garage-band origins to a Hendrix cover, a story-song about a man with a gun in his hand not unlike "Stagger Lee," whose lore extended across each new take as folk-rock itself developed into a Marshall-stacked, as in amplified, counterculture. The poet's gambit of Smith, with her ties to scruffy bohemian collector Harry Smith, oedipal playwright Sam Shepard, transgressive flower-fister Robert Mapplethorpe, was—in direct parallel to her axman Kaye's garage-rock singles collection *Nuggets*—to rhapsodize this seemingly minor heritage.[6]

"The way you play guitar makes me feel so, makes me feel so . . ."—it's a rapture, but a very New York one, to the cadence of minimalist tape cutups by Steve Reich, fannishness and distance—"masochistic." Venus in Furs, a Velvet Underground fan might mentally append; that kind of punk sex. "And Patti Hearst, you standing there in front of the Symbionese Liberation Army": one radical freeze-frame saluting another, befitting Mapplethorpe's photo of Smith as genderfucked Sinatra on the sleeve. "I was wondering, were you getting it every night from a black revolutionary man."

Oh, that.

Long since time we got back to that. One song we don't play much anymore—even the band skips it in concert—is "Brown Sugar" by the Rolling Stones, imagining themselves as slavers whipping Black women to explore their attraction to, let's spell it *rock 'n' roll*. Another is John Lennon's "Woman Is the N***** of the World," a white-man's burden of a counterculture anthem if ever there were one. And a third is the Patti Smith Group's "Rock N Roll N*****," written by Smith and Kaye, where in the rave-up the N-word features more often than "you ain't nothing" in you know what, and Black guitar feedback shaman Jimi Hendrix and white paint splatterer Jackson Pollock are equated as "outside of society," live'r than you'll ever be, as a Stones bootleg once put it. Is it possible that every white rock and roller with a formative attachment to "Hound Dog" by Elvis Presley, to the wail let loose in a studio and mastered onto a single, has a song like this in their catalog? (Lou

Reed: "I Wanna Be Black.") How extensively does whiteness in the guise of Frankenstein punk Blackness permeate every part of the wail? Constitute it? "Hey Joe" isn't even a screamer, not the full-force gale Smith was capable of. But the wail has been engrained, as her voice, even apart from lyrical exposition, conveys what it means to float unattached on a recording over sounds such as these: "I'm nobody's patsy anymore / and I feel so free."

The legacy of blackface minstrelsy, laughing at Black Americans for the worst reasons, had by the 1970s commingled with viewpoints like Norman Mailer's "The White Negro," valuing Black Americans for the worst reasons. But the whiteness of the rock and roll wail, the punk wail, had still more making it, to interpolate a single by the Electric Eels, "So Agitated." The Presley "Hound Dog" single was a traveling rebellion starter kit that arrived with no instructions. Following it, some rock and most punk singles became declarations that the performers were lifers, not dabblers. Maybe they had been privileged once, almost certainly if one considers any teen imaginary a privilege, but they were no richer than Big Mama Thornton now. They had let go. To return to Melville, once his whale epic tanked, this was the realm of the incestuous successor volume: *Pierre; or, The Ambiguities*.

And singles proved to be perfect containers for this usage, too. It wasn't easy to track down a self-released seven-inch like "Hey Joe" when I started playing songs over the college radio airwaves about a decade later—rarities were lifted from the station bins, so you had to track down punk sampler LPs or generate a tape cart. That remove from the original, the opposite of the ubiquity of a "Hound Dog," accrued to the single, became one of its characteristics. I doubt this was explicitly the project when Smith and Kaye put the song together, but I might be wrong: they met when Smith told Kaye, a record store clerk, how much she'd enjoyed his article on doo-wop record collectors. Like Lou Reed, another collector of vintage 45s, these rock and roll bohemians secured holy texts to complete their alchemical rituals.

By the time R.E.M. released their first single, at the start of the 1980s, marginality was a core part of the enchantment—they even called it "Radio Free Europe," comparing the act of putting out, from Athens, a song like Smith's "Hey Joe" to beaming anticommunist messages into controlled provinces of the Soviet Union. Yet Michael Stipe's voice was pointedly branded by the LP *Murmur*, which contained a version of the same song (just not *the* version). And R.E.M.'s connection to the Black wildness referenced by their heroes as a white wail was equally attenuated—Velvets covers, jangle-pop guitar. Stipe became more willing to sing out over time. His "don't fuck with me" in *Monster*, slipped into its single "What's the Frequency, Kenneth," reverberated queerness and glam. White wails, I might say with a nod to performance studies theorist (and Gun Club fan) José Esteban Muñoz, sought in claiming LGBTQ identity to become a variant of minoritarian disidentification.[7]

Which only made the Black punk road, never fully taken, all the more poignant, Lester Bangs on "White Noise Supremacists" notwithstanding. James Brown, who for a time defined a version of the wail as anything but white, inheriting a mantle and even some musicians from Little Richard, and who shared with Elvis Presley a flirtation with Richard Nixon and uneasiness around countercultures, wrote in his memoir, "A lot of people don't understand about the hollering I do. A man once came up to me in a hotel lobby and said, 'So you're James Brown. You make a million dollars, and all you do is scream and holler.' 'Yes,' I said very quiet, 'but I scream and holler on key.'"[8] The screams of Brown becoming Chuck D and Ice Cube were largely distinct, give or take a James Chance, from those of Presley becoming Joe Strummer and PJ Harvey (to throw some new names into this mix).

What, exactly, was the whiteness of the wail? I think it was a legacy, dating back to the pre–recording devices days of pot-banging, tub-thumping parades, the rituals of charivari that white people becoming a working class used as they "made the night hideous" in registering their disapproval.[9] James Brown screamed on key to serve a groove. Whites wailed out of the belief that they were still in a position to shake and rattle the public sphere. Nina Sun Eidsheim warns us, in *The Race of Sound*, against any ascription of sonic racial identity: all such assumptions are constructed. I am not suggesting white people inherently wailed differently than Black people. But voices are still socially regulated, often in racially defined ways, afforded different limits. Elvis shaking off his night as Steve Allen's butler. Patti Smith voicing the N-word like the door code to Iggy and his

Michigan friends' rock and roll speakeasy. Kurt Cobain's doomy final grunge howl on that MTV *Unplugged* appearance, unlike anything by his model Lead Belly. Much of an influential, gut-level valuation of rock at its most intense has depended on an ideal of loudness as an achievement, as resistance, its signature object the vinyl single as a wailing wall of sound. This has to be accounted for, even as the scream subsides, replaced by new rituals of semiprivileged precarity. Many of us heard the wail as the "Levitate Me" pinnacle of rock and roll (yeah, add the Pixies here, too)—red meat where a pop chorus was white sugar.

Elvis Presley was presented, for decades, as an acceptable plunderer of Big Mama Thornton because there was a secret place his voice, that dangling power line, could take you, a place where Patti Page was impolitely set aside. The white wail wasn't her whiteness; it also wasn't Blackness of any nonracist imagining. Greil Marcus, in more than one book (so I'll forgive myself for citing it in more than one book, too) quoted Neil Young to the effect that rock and roll felt older than country and blues.[10] Fleshing out the idea, tagging rock and roll as a return to blackface, that Scotty Moore "damn, n*****" I mentioned earlier, equates with how Nick Tosches wrote about the secret history and twisted roots of blackface minstrel Emmett Miller, whose barnyard yodel agitated the original "Lovesick Blues." We can find intervening examples of a sort: the move from communal groove to peer-group wildness in the white Original Dixieland Jazz Band; the New York–based folk scene at the Almanac Singers' Almanac

House, which in Robert Cantwell's telling was more like a *Hootenanny* in the sense of the album by the 1980s Replacements (add Paul Westerberg's wail to the list) than how we imagine Peter, Paul and Mary fans behaving.[11]

But the rock and roll single made the white wail louder than ever before—or since. Electrified instruments and magnetic tape produced a power surge: compare the acoustic early recordings of Muddy Waters with the moment "M-A-N" is spelled out on "Mannish Boy," as the band hammers down the period on each sentence. Again, there are no racial absolutes in music. But technology offered an affordance, and politics offered a caution: no outright messages allowed. In response, as George Lipsitz pointed out, what might have seemed like "nonsense syllables" offered a different SOS: "If one defines politics as the social struggle for a good life, then these songs represent politics of the highest order."[12]

An Elvis Presley "Hound Dog," achieved with the same studio tools and in the same political climate that produced Big Mama Thornton's original, and Muddy Waters' proclamation of manhood, cannot be viewed as identical to those loud wails. The divide, the schizophonia, was racial, whatever Presley's class origins in the partially integrated environments of mixed cheap housing, R&B radio broadcasts, clothing stores on Beale Street. Still, they were all records—singles on the loose, presumed dangerous. And if, as Springsteen said most clearly, Presley gave his white self the confidence to transform, then maybe we should see the world produced by the white wail at this moment as an answer in search of the right question, an answer designed to stop questions altogether. Not, What would it sound like "if I could find a white man with the Negro sound and the Negro feel"?, as Sun's Sam Phillips is said so often to have said (try Googling it), but, What would it mean to define rock and roll as "I don't sing like nobody," to rock all blues away and live where the needle scratched the vinyl?

True confessions part 3: I half-remember coming back from a record store in 1990 with some singles. One, on Merge Records out of collegiate North Carolina, was Superchunk's "Slack Motherfucker," with its constant screechy complaining tone building into a chiming three-note summation (*gong-gong-gong*) and polished chorus—disruptor concept to IPO launch, you might say in retrospect, thinking about the Research Triangle and Arcade Fire selling out Madison Square Garden while on Merge, but not one of us would have articulated it that way then. A second, on Sub Pop Records out of collegiate Washington, was Nirvana's "Sliver": a recollection of childhood, parents away for date night, left with the grandparents, disturbed for no specified reason, and screaming—on key, the key of what turned out to be future record sales—"Grandma take me home."

Do a Web search and compare the two picture-sleeve covers: not band photos but art images of otherness, summoning alien as in alienated not-quite-humans, the punk rocker as creep, as what Cobain would famously sum up—mulatto, albino, mosquito, libido.

There was nothing especially remarkable about this. It's there in the poster for the night Mudhoney opened for Sonic Youth at the Fillmore West in 1988, white people with their eyes X-ed out, or the cover of the seven-inch single that same founding Sub Pop grunge band was touring on, "Touch Me I'm Sick." Toilet-bowl image but serene typeface and trim—passive-aggressive hype mode of a label conceiving "World Domination." Something inchoate in Elvis Presley's "Hound Dog" had become the Amerindie version of the punk version of the rock and roll single. Wailers and Sonics, garage-rock legends, went back in the Pacific Northwest to before the Beatles. Mudhoney knew that history record by record. But their singer Mark Arm proved incapable, onstage during the first Pop Conference in 2002, of analyzing it. The impulse to inquire had been discarded—only a sound remained. And perhaps shame—over the Blackness X-ed out multiple times?

Which leads to a follow-up question: Was the white wail a noun or a verb? I refer to the chapter "Swing—From Verb to Noun" in the Amiri Baraka (then LeRoi Jones) classic *Blues People: Negro Music in White America*. Baraka noted how records let a middle-class, middle-American white player, Bix Beiderbecke, hang on the wall of jazz icons not far from New Orleans and blues-steeped Louis Armstrong. Complexities in the argument mirrored the differences between an Elvis Presley inciting teenage riot and Sonic Youth as much theorizing as performing "Teenage Riot" on *Daydream Nation*—in *Blues People*, Baraka contrasted working-class Black blues culture and the college-educated Black players

(Duke Ellington, Coleman Hawkins, Fletcher Henderson) who first made big band jazz. The result, though, come Benny Goodman, forecast rock and roll—a white jackpot built on uncoupling a sound genre from the culture of Black collective creativity. "Swing music, which was the result of arranged big-band jazz, as it developed to a music that had almost nothing to do with blues, had very little to do with black America, though that is certainly where it had come from."[13]

Writing as part of the new jazz studies in the 1990s, another poet-critic, Nathaniel Mackey, reworked Baraka's viewpoint in "Other: From Noun to Verb." While white domination put Black creativity in one fixed place, Mackey looked for methods of Black "othering"—modeled on Jamaican versioning, like dub remixes—that resisted. John Coltrane's take on an older song. Zora Neale Hurston's vernacular storytellers. The fugitive spirit of Ishmael Reed and Toni Morrison. Thelonious Monk and bebop as the response to swing, the move back from noun to verb. At the end, confronting that bastion of re-noun for renown, neo-traditionalism, embodied by Wynton Marsalis, Mackey threw out as an ideal the idea that the verb-iage of an experimentalist such as Henry Threadgill should be fully recognized alongside working-class Blackness. In vital ways Mackey's vision was realized as time passed. Black authorship, from writers to performers, stressed the epistemological aside alongside the collective groove. Threadgill's Pulitzer followed Marsalis's.

With Baraka's statement, and Mackey's revision, clarifying the question, then: Where in the noun-to-verb spectrum should we locate the white wail? That relocating scream is an act (verb), or at least a fervent performance of inaction (stifled verb), that summons a place (noun) that is primarily audible (a noun that can't be owned, only reached via an exotic journey). Yowza. Remember Giddins on Art Pepper and the idea of the white wail as, at core, a personal search fraught with peril. Elvis Presley, Kurt Cobain, a more recent figure such as Swedish-American emo-inflected Soundcloud rapper Lil Peep: these singers and many others can be viewed through a lens of drugs moved from worthwhile risk to unstoppable disaster, of stardom consumed, leaving nothing else to mainline. Subcultures love such allegories of commodification, like the fanzine devoted to white wails, *Maximum Rocknroll*, which after Cobain's suicide showed an image of a dude, gun in his mouth, with the headline "Major Labels: Some of Your Friends Are Already This Fucked." But that would leave out race, in a moment when even what's left of MRR shreds itself to pieces over white punk identity.[14] Better, in the vein of Giddins, to wonder if a noun, in this case the Elvis "Hound Dog" single, produced a verb—a life spent working through the implications of being caught in its trap, unable (as Alice Walker fantasized in "Nineteen Fifty-Five") to resolve its irreducibly problematic status. Perhaps every successive white wail reproduces this dynamic, one anguished and cherished convulsion at a time.

I talked to Patterson Hood about these songs because he'd been there and back. His dad, David Hood, was a white bass player in a recording studio team (the Muscle Shoals Rhythm Section) renowned for playing grooving "Black" music—his succulent "I'll Take You There" bassline came up when you reached his answering machine. Patterson was next generation, a punk and indie rock kid in Alabama, then off to that mecca Athens, where he and his partner, Mike Cooley, made the Drive-By Truckers out of songs about bulldozers and dirt, bubbas with AIDS, and a concept album, *Southern Rock Opera*, about the cultural legacy of Lynyrd Skynyrd. Patterson likes Bruce Springsteen more than I do, hears his own wail as something other than white—maybe whiteness in an appreciative relationship to Blackness, like Elvis losing himself in a Little Richard cover. Premises that, as a critic, I can challenge but that can be lived honorably, however open to question.

The day we Zoomed, he was wrapping the mix on an album recorded with his dad; Jim Dickinson (godfather Memphis producer of indie legends Big Star); and Jim Dickinson's kids—Hoods and Dickinsons to go around, tapes still being worked on years after Jim's death. Next, he had a Truckers arena date in Montana, then what they call a "Dimmer Twins" set with Cooley at Newport Folk Festival. He might never make it as big as those Glimmer Twins his dad worked with—Mick Jagger and Keith Richards—or even his one-time bandmate, Jason Isbell, and Brittany Howard, the Black woman rocker he'd so fervently encouraged. He stayed a verb, in motion, active in a culture his music half-created. The song of his that stayed pivotal for him, "The Living Bubba," had as its refrain, "I can't die now 'cause I got another show to do."

Patterson's involved relationship to music means more than any abstract relationship. When I brought up the R.E.M. and Patti Smith tribute to the Stooges at the Rock Hall of Fame induction, he lit up. "I was at the rehearsals for that!" It was a big moment for a longtime Athens resident: guitarist (and former record store clerk) Peter Buck, as part of their growing relationship, had invited him to watch a band known for its insularity prep one last gig. There was no question why the two groups had covered the Stooges, Patterson said: to make the case for their induction, which followed in 2010.

I asked how he compared his and my cohort's quest for that kind of canon reshaping with the newer efforts to hail Big Mama Thornton and all the Black women pioneers.

> That's the age we are. That's what we came up in. It's not really fair to hold ourselves accountable for not being more aware yet, when we were younger, of something that happened ten years before you and I were born. As lovers of rock and roll history, sure, we eventually got there and saw the importance of that. But when we were kids growing up that was too long ago for us to have been able to wrap our heads around. We were in the heat of the battle that we were in, for the rock and roll of our age and our generation. Granted, the Stooges came along a little before you and I, before our time, too. That's why it's so great that R.E.M. and Patti Smith did

> that. And that's why it's great that now people are digging deeper and recognizing Big Mama Thornton and the early pioneers, particularly those of color and those that were women.

A strong answer, but it didn't solve anything. "I don't know. Our society is still so segregated." He recalled WLAY in his hometown playing a big mix of Black music, white music, country music. "They probably did play the Big Mama Thornton version—at least at night. And they did play the Elvis version. And I'm sure they played 'Doggie in the Window,' too." How about "I Wanna Be Your Dog"? "No, I never heard 'I Wanna Be Your Dog' on the radio growing up." The whiteness of the wail? "I try to not be overly self-conscious when I'm singing. Sixty-five to 70 percent of the singers that most influenced me were either Black singers or white singers that were very influenced by Black singers." He gets back to the family business: "And a lot of those singers, a lot of those records, had white guys playing on them, too. I grew up in that."

My relationship to music, as (to toss off a few nouns) a rock critic and magazine editor, a college professor and author of university-press histories, a homeowner in many a gentrifying neighborhood, has been far more passive than Patterson's, save for one period: when I was a college radio DJ, playing vinyl records over the airwaves and talking into the void. When I heard a piece of music in those days, my first as a deeply active listener, ransacking the station library at all hours, I was imagining myself getting to play it, how it would sound shooting out after the previous song. My sense of music, then, was caught up in the feeling of holding a slip-cued record in place with my left hand while the turntable spun underneath it, waiting for the moment I'd release it and let the thing go man go. Spinning, the noun, the record, became a verb. The song became part of a set. It was still, in a reverse way, schizophonic: I was cut off not from the source of my sound but from my listeners, unable to know how they were reacting—the most frequent station callers wanted "'My Way' by Sid Vicious." But from inside a record, inside a station, I was playing music. Iggy Pop!

# Outro

**THERE IS A SMALL PERFORMANCE SPACE** in East Nashville, where I have lived the past few years, the East Room, attached to a shop, Hail, that sells weird stuff—a goth boutique. One night at the East Room, we went to see Olivia Scibelli and her band Idle Bloom play, because we hadn't yet, and Olivia is amazing: makes money cutting hair, donates time to Southern Girls Rock Camp, helped start an all-ages space, Drkmttr, not long after this story took place, that during COVID hosted the Nashville Free Store. As for Idle Bloom: ah, that sound. Superchunk encapsulated this vibe with their song "My Noise":

*It rides beside me*
*It has no choice*
*It's my life*
*It is my voice*
*It is stupid*
*It is my noise.*

Idle Bloom sounded like that to me, like the kind of group I would have played on the radio in the 1980s alongside, say, Scrawl and Death of Samantha.

But Idle Bloom weren't headlining. Soccer Mommy took that slot because they were all over the airwaves. Okay, one station, but a pretty big one: SiriusXMU, the closest thing satellite radio offered to college radio. (These days, you could add WNXP in Nashville, a community station with a Soccer Mommy–oriented format.) As a station, XMU was still far too white in its programming but made it a point to play women artists, far more than had been the case in my era. Like then-twenty-year-old Sophie Allison, Soccer Mommy's leader. Allison was Nashville raised and signed to the southern indie Fat Possum Records, though she attended New York University for a time and knows hipster Brooklyn. Talking to our still-extant alt-weekly, the *Nashville Scene*, she recalled the frustrations of a punk community where "every show I went to had five bands with all dudes. It made me ask, 'Is this really all that's here? Is this it?'" So she learned to record her songs at home on a Tascam cassette deck. The old story: if you could bring a song, sound, and attitude to life on a record, that was a big step forward in striving for the same in the outside world.[1]

But I also see Allison as part of something newer, the Rock 'n' Roll Camp for Girls universe, with its genius enticement: start a band with fellow campers, and in one week you'll write a song together and learn to play it well enough that you can perform it in some cool club during the weekend showcase. The Willie Mae Rock Camp in Brooklyn, it should be noted again, is named for Willie Mae (Big Mama) Thornton. But the origins of rock camp were neither Black nor southern: the idea originated in 2001 in the Pacific Northwest, where riot grrrl bands had done so much to seize the wail across gender lines: think of Sleater-Kinney's Corin Tucker, summoning gods in "I Wanna Be Your Joey Ramone" ("Pictures of me on your bedroom door . . . I'm the queen of rock and roll"). Ultimately, riot grrrls would find themselves rueful about racial lines they hadn't thought to challenge. Rock camp was a subset, initially, of what Fred Armisen and another Sleater member, guitarist Carrie Brownstein, called *Portlandia* in their sitcom of hipster gentrification. That's an old story, time enough for former campers to become counselors, then start grown-up bands.

As our family switched cities, I watched my daughter go through rock camp a time or three, mentored briefly by former Hole drummer Patty Schemel in Los Angeles, finding a hero in the late Jessi Zazu of Those Darlins in Music City, eventually drumming in an all-ages band, Dudette. Bebe's own tastes are neither Olivia's nor mine, pointing out some of the places in the story of the wail that this book won't get to. When you ask her about screamers, she'll namedrop Slipknot's "Eyeless" and "Pulse of the Maggots," Avenged Sevenfold's "Burn It Down" and "Scream," In This Moment's "Big Bad Wolf," Periphery's "Blood Eagle," and Beartooth's "Rock Is Dead."

But the Rock Camp approach favored something closer to what Soccer Mommy do: verse, chorus, bridge, a diaristic lyric and some goofy attitude in close competition with some vulnerability. Like Soccer Mommy's first single. Electric guitar of the dreamy sort you get when Pixies are your camp's folk music. Drums of the kind that Bebe broke down for me immediately: "It's just the rock beat, dad." High-pitched and probably multitracked (Patti Page–style) vocals, more breathy than aggressive, because the anger is best served cold, and structures of feeling shift with new cohorts. Caught on tape, on whatever we call the file it's caught on these days, Sophie Allison sings a first line that can be this book's last line: *"I don't want to be your fucking dog."*

# ACKNOWLEDGMENTS

This book came together quickly, but its roots are in years of teaching, writing, and conferencing: earworms for bookworms. At the University of Alabama, where students respond to a bluesy growl and guitar in ways no amount of Irving Berlin or Neutral Milk Hotel can match, I have long taught an American pop survey, now two semesters long, that keeps every era of US popular music ringing permanently in my ears. Thanks to everyone who ever took the class and came to understand its pedagogical hook: that moment in between hearing a song, or a couple contrasted, and trying to find the words to account for what just hit you. Getting to live in that moment for a living is a privilege I don't take lightly.

*Songbooks*, my most recent book, a long read with many short takes on the literature of American music, made this one a perfect palate cleanser, a short read with an extended take on the entry on Elvis Presley books there. Thanks to Joshua Clover and Emily Lordi for welcoming me to the Singles series, Joshua in particular for his thematic rigor and copy queries credited to "Jane" in the tracked changes, a small nod to twenty-five years back when I was editing him at the *Village Voice* and he was still writing under the name Jane Dark. Those were different times (to cite a band he hates). Thanks as ever to Ken Wissoker at Duke, whose groove is more relaxed than any version of "Hound Dog" but who very well may know some dusty take I have missed.

I first presented on Patti Page, my way of turning the "Hound Dog" tug-of-war between Big Mama Thornton and Elvis Presley into a game of rock-paper-scissors, at the Pop Conference, which I founded and co-organized for many years. That's really the underpinning of this book intellectually, trying to put the ideas of one set of my conference colleagues, upending canons and assumptions to emphasize Black artistry and multiplicity, into a conversation with another set prone to make learned Silly Putty of pop recordings, viewing them as category warpers altogether. Thanks to all who Pop Conference, in person and in spirit.

This kid from Queens never imagined he'd wind up in the South, but an early hint of what was to come came at the Haunted Hillbilly Hoedown in Pittsburgh in 1999. I attended on a whim with my wife, Ann Powers, nonpareil turner of tables as both writer and cultural instigator, not to mention the person I not only love but most want to whisper words into the ears of at concerts. We were privileged that weekend to first hear the Alabama band Drive-By Truckers, then rushed home to write about the best unsigned band we'd ever encountered. It has been one of life's treasures to befriend their leader, Patterson Hood, over the years, and I thank him for agreeing to be my occasional interlocutor here.

Present, too, I'm happy to note, supplying her list of wailers from the Octane-Turbo-Liquid Metal portion of the SiriusXM dial, is our daughter, Bebe, a southerner since kindergarten who once took part in a performance of Alabama music classics at Tuscaloosa Magnet Schools—Elementary; she sang "Heat Wave"—where do you think Martha Reeves is from?—and another kid tackled "Hound Dog." Frank N. Furter Nietzsche Weisbard, named for the star of Bebe's beloved *Rocky Horror Picture Show* and her favorite author, has been her high school support animal. Frankie will be our support animal now, as Bebe heads north to college and we all try to live in Nashville without her. That kid rocks.

# NOTES

## Intro

1. Lott, *Love and Theft*.

2. For the two lists, see https://www.rollingstone.com/music/music-lists/500-greatest-songs-of-all-time-151127/ and https://www.rollingstone.com/music/music-lists/best-songs-of-all-time-1224767/ (accessed October 27, 2022).

3. Cohn, *Awopbopaloobop Alopbamboom*; Marcus, *Mystery Train*; and Lester Bangs, "How Long Will We Care?," *Village Voice*, August 29, 1977 (collected as Bangs, "Where Were You When Elvis Died?"). Marcus's book, first published in 1975, has had many subsequent editions, each updating the story in a "Notes and Discographies" section. Marcus returned to Elvis in his books *Dead Elvis* and *Double Trouble*. Presley also appeared frequently in a recurring column by Marcus, collected as Marcus, *Real Life Rock*.

4. Steptoe, "Big Mama Thornton," 55–56 . Steptoe cites Halberstam's "Queer Voices and Musical Genders."

5. Mahon, *Black Diamond Queens*, 29–51 (quotes: 29–30, 38, 39, 47–48); and Leiber and Stoller, *Hound Dog*, 93–96.

6. Lott, *Love and Theft*, 56.

7. Fink, "Elvis Everywhere," 170.

## Chapter 1. "Doggie in the Window" and the 1950s Pop Single

1. Dylan, in *No Direction Home* (Paramount Pictures, 2005); *Theme Time Radio Hour*, season 1, episode 16, "Dogs," aired August 16, 2006, on XM Satellite Radio; and Patterson Hood, interview by author, July 16, 2021.

2. Page, "There Are Two Sides to a Song."

3. "Country Music Is Big Business and Nashville Is Its Detroit," *Newsweek*, August 11, 1952; and Lange, *Smile When You Call Me a Hillbilly*, 61.

4. Weisbard, *Top 40 Democracy*.

5. Gillett, *Sound of the City*; and Peterson, "Why 1955?"

6. Ramsey, *Race Music*, 44–75 (quote: 50); and Broven, *Record Makers and Breakers*, 21–32.

7. Keightley, "'You Keep Coming Back Like a Song'" (quotes: 18, 19, 20, 22).

8. Waksman, *Instruments of Desire*, 36–74 (quotes: 37–39).

9. Quoted in Zak, *I Don't Sound Like Nobody*, 59.

10. Zak, *I Don't Sound Like Nobody*, 119, 168.

11. Page, *This Is My Song*, 7–45 (quotes: 7, 23–24, 36–37).

12. Page, *This Is My Song*, 55–65 (quote: 61).

13. Page, *This Is My Song*, 66–78 (quote: 73).

14. Page, *This Is My Song*, 78–170 (quote: 80).

15. Page, *This Is My Song*, 170–272 (quote: 221); *The Patti Page Video Songbook*, DVD (View Video, 2004).

16. Schoemer, *Great Pretenders* (quotes: 21, 23, 28, 29).

17. For more, see Broven, *Record Makers and Breakers*, 101–2.

## Chapter 2. Dog Ditties

1. Writing on Stephen Foster and blackface minstrelsy is surveyed in Weisbard, *Songbooks*, 22–24, 39–42, 334–37. W. T. Lhamon, between his study *Raising Cain* and his analysis and collection of Thomas Rice's work, *Jump Jim Crow*, parses the initial blackface wave. Eric Lott's *Love and Theft* is the central cultural studies interpretation of minstrelsy, including much on Foster. For Carson, see Huber, *Linthead Stomp*. For Crosby, see Gary Giddins's still-emerging but now two-volume biography *Bing Crosby*.

2. For spirituals as pop and roots combined, see Graham, *Spirituals*; along with Cruz, *Culture on the Margins*, on "ethnosympathy"; and the genealogies in Radano, *Lying Up a Nation*. See Handy, *Father of the Blues*; for his impact, see Mack, *Fictional Blues*; Dore, *Novel Sounds*; and the scene where he keeps Dorothy Scarborough waiting in Hamilton, *In Search of the Blues*, 89–90. For Bourbon Street and New Orleans, see Hersch, *Subversive Sounds*; for Beale, see McKee and Chisenhall, *Beale Black and Blue*; for Decatur Street, see Hunter, "'Sexual Pantomimes.'"

3. For ragtime writing, see the overview in Weisbard, *Songbooks*, 111–17; and Gilbert, *Product of Our Souls*. Touring shows are documented by Lynn Abbott and Doug Seroff, especially in *Ragged but Right*; as an interpretation, see McGinley, *Staging the Blues*. For "Crazy Blues," three disparate sources add detail and perspective: Miller, *Segregating Sound*, 187–214, which takes the story into "down-home" recording; Brooks,

*Liner Notes for the Revolution*, 380–87, on Black women's positional radicalism; and Young, *Grey Album*, 159–64, which revels in its modernity—"You say *Waste Land*, I say 'Crazy Blues'" (159).

4. For the 1920s pop industry, see Barnett, *Record Cultures*. For Duke Ellington, see Tucker, *Duke Ellington Reader*; along with Cohen, *Duke Ellington's America*; Edwards, "Literary Ellington"; and Vogel, *Scene of Harlem Cabaret*. For musicals, see Mast, *Can't Help Singin'*; Knapp, Morris, and Wolf, *Oxford Handbook of the American Musical*; and Maslon, *Broadway to Main Street*. For Al Jolson, see Rogin, *Blackface, White Noise*; and Most, *Making Americans*. For radio, see Hilmes, *Only Connect*. For crooners, see McCracken, *Real Men Don't Sing*; and Kaye, *You Call It Madness*. For Nashville and Jimmie Rodgers, see Stimeling, *Oxford Handbook of Country Music*; Mazor, *Meeting Jimmie Rodgers*; and Neal, *Songs of Jimmie Rodgers*. On the new recording technology globally, see Denning, *Noise Uprising*.

5. For record sales dwindling and responses, see Barnett, *Record Cultures*, 192–229; and Kenney, *Recorded Music in American Life*. For Crosby's triumph, see McCracken, *Real Men Don't Sing*; and Giddins, *Bing Crosby*, vol. 1, *A Pocketful of Dreams*. Robert Cantwell analyzes the Almanac Singers as bohemian rousers in *When We Were Good*. The overall story of the Popular Front is reclaimed by Michael Denning in *The Cultural Front*.

6. Erenberg, *Swingin' the Dream*, 35–64.

7. For writing on Sinatra, see Weisbard, *Songbooks*, 284–87. His relationship to the Popular Front registers in Denning, *Cultural Front*. His early pop impact absorbs Kahn, *Voice*; and Petkov and Mustazza, *Frank Sinatra Reader*. James Kaplan's biography, *The Voice*, is best on the early years.

8. Gregory, *Southern Diaspora*; and Daniel, *Lost Revolutions*. For honkytonk, see Malone, *Country Music USA*. Guitars get loud in Palmer, "Church of the Sonic Guitar," leading to his *Rock and Roll* and *Blues and Chaos*; for Mahalia Jackson, see Burford, *Mahalia Jackson and the Gospel Field*; for labels, see Broven, *Record Makers and Breakers*.

9. George Lipsitz makes this argument, about straightforward radicalism and sonic/expressive kinds, in "'Ain't Nobody Here but Us Chickens': The Class Origins of Rock and Roll," in *Rainbow at Midnight*, 303–33.

10. Eberly, *Music in the Air*; Sanjek, *Pennies from Heaven*; and Ennis, *Seventh Stream*. For jazz into jump blues, see DeVeaux, *Birth of Bebop*; and Ake, "Jazz Historiography and the Problem of Louis Jordan," in *Jazz Cultures*, 42–61.

11. Keightley, "'You Keep Coming Back Like a Song'" (Sinatra telegram: 35); Keightley, "Long Play"; Keightley, "Music for Middlebrows"; E. Wald, *How the Beatles Destroyed Rock 'n' Roll*; and Yagoda, *B Side*.

## Chapter 3. "Hound Dog," Take One: Big Mama Thornton

1. Nate Sloan and Charlie Harding, "Elvis, Big Mama Thornton, Doja Cat, and the Long Legacy of 'Hound Dog,'" *Switched on Pop* (podcast), July 26, 2022, https://switchedonpop.com/episodes/elvis-hound-dog-doja-cat-vegas-big-mama-thorton; and Hood, interview.

2. Leiber and Stoller, *Hound Dog*; Spörke, *Big Mama Thornton*; Steptoe, "Big Mama Thornton"; and Mahon, *Black Diamond Queens*, 29–51. For Robey, see Broven, *Record Makers and Breakers*; and Salem, *Late Great Johnny Ace*. The quote from Otis is from his *Listen to the Lambs*, quoted in Lipsitz, *Midnight at the Barrelhouse*, xxviii; see also Otis, *Upside Your Head!*

3. Halberstam, *Female Masculinity*; and Mahon, "Listening for Willie Mae 'Big Mama' Thornton's Voice," 1.

4. McCracken, *Real Men Don't Sing*.

5. Quoted in Ralph J. Gleason, "Big Mama Sings the Blues She Likes," liner notes, *Big Mama Thornton and the Chicago Blues Band*, vol. 2 (Arhoolie Records, 1967), quoted in Mahon, *Black Diamond Queens*, 36.

6. Spörke, *Big Mama Thornton*, 7–10 (quote: 7); and Hunter, "'Sexual Pantomimes.'"

7. Wilson, quoted in Stearns and Stearns, *Jazz Dance*, 24; and Hunter, "'Sexual Pantomimes,'" 159.

8. Lipsitz, "Introduction," xxvii, xxxiii–xxxiv.

9. Preston Lauterbach, "Sympathy for the Devil," *Oxford American*, Winter 2014, https://main.oxfordamerican.org/magazine/item/1040-sympathy-for-the-devil.

10. Johnson, quoted in Salem, *Late Great Johnny Ace*, 79–80 (ad: 82).

11. Leiber and Stoller, *Hound Dog* (quotes: 61–63); and Otis, quoted in Lipsitz, *Midnight at the Barrelhouse*, 42.

12. Lipsitz, *Midnight at the Barrelhouse*, 54, 55.

13. Small, *Musicking*; and Bruno, "'Is That All There Is?'"

14. Spörke, *Big Mama Thornton*, 146.

15. Decker, *Who Should Sing "Ol' Man River"?*

16. Playlist research courtesy of YouTube (https://www.youtube.com/results?search_query=%22lucky+old+sun%22) and Spotify (https://open.spotify.com/search/Lucky%20old%20sun/tracks).

17. Dylan, *Chronicles*, 107–41; Dove, quoted in Spörke, *Big Mama Thornton*, 87; Don Heck-

man, "Big Mama's 'Hound Dog,'" *New York Times*, January 4, 1970; and John Morthland, record review of *Stronger Than Dirt*, *Rolling Stone*, November 1, 1969, available at https://www.rocksbackpages.com/Library/Article/big-mama-thornton-istronger-than-dirti-mercury.

18. Gurley, quoted in Spörke, *Big Mama Thornton*, 69.

19. Steptoe, "Jody's Got Your Girl and Gone"; and Steptoe, "Big Mama Thornton," 55, 57.

20. Mack, *Fictional Blues*, 67–107; Mahon, "Listening for Willie Mae 'Big Mama' Thornton's Voice," 4; and Spörke, *Big Mama Thornton*, 144.

21. Nate Sloan and Charlie Harding, "Elvis, Big Mama Thornton, Doja Cat, and the Long Legacy of 'Hound Dog.'"

## Chapter 4. Elvis Presley Belatedly Records "Hound Dog"

1. Thornton, quoted in Mack, *Fictional Blues*, 90–91; Moore, quoted in Spörke, *Big Mama Thornton*, 34–36.

2. Hood, interview. For Presley's biography, see Guralnick, *Last Train to Memphis*. Footage of Presley on Milton Berle's show on June 5, 1956, is widely available on YouTube, for example, here: "Elvis—'Hound Dog' and Dialogue—Milton Berle Show—5 June 1956," YouTube video, 7:53, https://www.youtube.com/watch?v=WJnVQDA9rHA.

3. Guralnick, *Last Train to Memphis*, 277–304 (media reactions and Presley response: 285–86); Bertrand, *Race, Rock, and Elvis* (*Charlotte Observer*: 103).

4. Guralnick, *Last Train to Memphis*, 277–304. Footage of Presley on *The Steve Allen Show* on July 1, 1956, is also available on YouTube: "*The Steve Allen Show* 07/01/1956," YouTube video, 58:23, https://www.youtube.com/watch?v=Em3ON9UfS74.

5. Guralnick, *Last Train to Memphis*, 297; Bertrand, *Race, Rock and Elvis*, 242.

6. Guralnick, *Last Train to Memphis*, 297–99 ("national anthem": 431).

7. Guralnick, *Last Train to Memphis* (quotes: 297, 300).

8. Presley's three 1956–57 appearances on *The Ed Sullivan Show* are collected on a DVD set, *The 3 Complete Ed Sullivan Shows Starring Elvis Presley: Including Other Artists, Commercials and More* (Sofa, 2018).

9. For the 1968 performance on DVD, see *Elvis '68 Comeback: Special Edition* (Sony Legacy, 2006); for the 1970 performance, see "Elvis Presley—'Hound Dog' (Live in Las Vegas—1970)," YouTube video, 1:52, https://www.youtube.com/watch?v=ptmHdzaduL4; for the June 19, 1977, Omaha performance

clip, aired posthumously as *Elvis in Concert*, see "Elvis Presley Hound Dog Omaha 1977," YouTube video, 1:43, https://www.youtube.com/watch?v=lzyIu91jPjc (accessed December 22, 2022).

10. Marcus, *Mystery Train* (Marcus-Dylan discussion: 231, 2020 ed.); Walker, "Nineteen Fifty-Five," 15; and Mahon, *Black Diamond Queens*, 39.

11. Guralnick, *Last Train to Memphis*, 131.

12. Spörke, *Big Mama Thornton*, 7, quoting Ralph Gleason, "Big Mama Sings the Blues She Likes," *San Francisco Chronicle*, April 6, 1970; and Mahon, *Black Diamond Queens*, 29 (quoting Shaw: 108).

13. Zak, *I Don't Sound Like Nobody*; Johnson, *Elvis Presley Speaks!* (quote: 7) ; and Hopkins, *Elvis*, 54.

14. Zak, *I Don't Sound Like Nobody* (quotes, including Howe and Race: 158, 166–68.

## Chapter 5. "Hound Dog" as Influence

1. R. Ellison, *Invisible Man*, 8.

2. John, *Me*, 9–10.

3. Richards, *Life*, 56.

4. For Lennon in 1965, the less-than-firm sourcing goes: August 28, 1965, statement after meeting Elvis Presley, quoted in Wayne, *Leading Men of MGM*, 386; also partly quoted in Davies, *Beatles*, 19. For the other quotes, see Wenner, *Lennon Remembers*, 18; The Beatles, *Beatles Anthology*, 11; and John Lennon, interview by David Sheff, *Playboy*, January 1981, published in full as Lennon and Ono, *All We Are Saying*, 101.

5. "Live at Madison Square Garden | Hound Dog," YouTube video, 3:35, https://www.youtube.com/watch?v=Wt5Ar7XQR9I (accessed October 31, 2022).

6. "Bruce Springsteen's Eulogy for Clarence Clemons," *Rolling Stone*, June 29, 2011, https://www.rollingstone.com/music/music-news/bruce-springsteens-eulogy-for-clarence-clemons-62867/. Connections among *Nuggets* garage band songs, arena rock, and punk are discussed in Waksman, *This Ain't the Summer of Love*, ch. 1. For Springsteen's "Hound Dog" at the Stone Pony, see "Hound Dog—Bruce Springsteen (23–07–1989 The Stone Pony, Asbury Park, New Jersey)," audio only (with Little Richard–style intro included), YouTube video, 3:20, https://www.youtube.com/watch?v=mMmGNgJy1rk; and "Hound Dog" ( intro truncated), YouTube video, 3:24, https://www.youtube.com/watch?v=mYNmBYbaq4U. For the Little Richard clip from Granada TV's *Don't Knock the Rock* with Sounds Incorporated backing him and the Shirelles perhaps going through the motions, too, see "Little Richard—'Hound

Dog' (Rare)," YouTube video, 4:30, https://www.youtube.com/watch?v=xbHC54c4AR4.

7. Bruce Springsteen, "Exclusive: The Complete Text of Bruce Springsteen's SXSW Keynote Address," *Rolling Stone*, March 28, 2012, https://www.rollingstone.com/music/music-news/exclusive-the-complete-text-of-bruce-springsteens-sxsw-keynote-address-86379/; Springsteen, *Born to Run*, 39–41 (quotes: 39); and "Which Eight Songs Would Bruce Springsteen Take to a Desert Island?," *Desert Island Discs*, BBC Radio 4, https://www.bbc.co.uk/programmes/articles/9FNJXs9HzJhV6jZ4rMCKN3/which-eight-songs-would-bruce-springsteen-take-to-a-desert-island (accessed December 21, 2022).

8. *Us*, "The King and I," August 24, 1987.

9. Mars on *Arsenio Hall* in 1991: "Bruno Mars Six Year Old Elvis Impersonator vs Dancing Grannies in 1991 Rare," YouTube video, 2:38, https://www.youtube.com/watch?v=wF1Jxsuhkhw; and Mars in the 1990 documentary *Viva Elvis*: "Bruno Mars Aged 4: World's Youngest Elvis Impersonator (Full Interview)," YouTube video, 3:32, https://www.youtube.com/watch?v=tdxr0z3SZ74.

10. Robert Christgau: Dean of American Rock Critics, "Eric Clapton," http://robertchristgau.com/get_artist.php?name=Eric+Clapton (accessed December 21, 2022).

11. VHS (Films Media Group, 1984); DVD (Films for the Humanities & Sciences, 2003); YouTube, "Big Mama Thornton 1984: Rooster Blues / Ball & Chain - Hound Dog (Legends of Rhythm & Blues -7+8)," 11:07, https://www.youtube.com/watch?v=nWE8Cd4yIMs (accessed December 21, 2022).

12. G. Wald, "'Have a Little Talk.'"

13. Moten, *In the Break*.

14. "Laurie Anderson on Letterman, May 8, 1984," YouTube video, 7:18, https://www.youtube.com/watch?v=p46nOuCVnYc; Laurie Anderson, holding dog, and Lou Reed on *Charlie Rose*, July 8, 2003: "Laurie Anderson and Lou Reed Interviewed by Charlie Rose (2003)—Part One," YouTube video, 13:40, https://www.youtube.com/watch?v=W-LFd-PQd6E; and "Laurie Anderson and Lou Reed Interviewed by Charlie Rose (2003)—Part Two," YouTube video, 13:20, https://www.youtube.com/watch?v=iQWiyKtMemo.

15. Laurie Anderson, "Norton Lecture 1: The River | Laurie Anderson: Spending the War without You," recorded February 10, 2021, YouTube video, 1:43:01, https://www.youtube.com/watch?v=6LuKgGn5e2g.

## Chapter Six. Interpreting "Hound Dog"

1. Blesh, *Shining Trumpets*, 378–89; and Charters, *Elvis Presley Calls His Mother*, 1. For

an overview of books on Elvis Presley, see Weisbard, *Songbooks*, 339–44.

2. Goldman, *Elvis* (quotes: 118, 125, 532); and Stearns, *Story of Jazz*, 107.

3. Cohn, *Pop from the Beginning*; *Rock from the Beginning*; *Awopbopaloobop Alopbamboom: Pop from the Beginning*; and *Awopbopaloobop Alopbamboom: The Golden Age of Rock* (quotes: 23, 104); and Peellaert and Cohn, *Rock Dreams* (quote: n.p.).

4. Booth, *True Adventures of the Rolling Stones*. Booth's "Hound Dog to the Manor Born," was reprinted as "Situation Report" in *Rythm Oil* (Ford exchange: 182–83).

5. Marcus, *Dead Elvis*, 65.

6. Marcus, *Double Trouble*, 183; Marcus, *Like a Rolling Stone*; and Hall and Jefferson, *Resistance through Rituals*; Thompson, *Making of the English Working Class* .

7. Marcus, *Mystery Train* ("Hound Dog" discussed: 13, 190, 196, 202; quotes: 206, 419, 422, 426, and 426n).

8. Marcus, *Mystery Train*, 202–4, 420–27.

9. Bangs, "How Long Will We Care?," collected as Bangs, "Where Were You When Elvis Died?"

10. Fink, "Elvis Everywhere" (quotes: 164, 173).

11. Comentale, *Sweet Air* (quotes: 162, 170, 171–72, 172, and 174).

12. Bertrand, *Race, Rock, and Elvis* (false Presley quote: 219).

## Chapter 7. The Whiteness of the Wail

1. Giddins, "Whiteness of the Wail," in *Riding on a Blue Note*, 254; and Kun, *Audiotopia*, 51–52.

2. "I Wanna Be Your Dog / 1969," Rate Your Music, https://rateyourmusic.com/release/single/the-stooges/i-wanna-be-your-dog-1969/ (accessed November 3, 2022); and "The Stooges 'I Wanna Be Your Dog' (Mono) Single Promo 1969," 2013 collection remaster, YouTube video, 2:40, https://www.youtube.com/watch?v=E5nf_Q_7U64.

3. Iggy Pop, interview by Carl Wilson, Red Bull Music Academy, Ludger-Duvernay Theatre, September 26, 2016, https://www.redbullmusicacademy.com/lectures/iggy-pop-lecture.

4. "Sonic Youth—'I Wanna Be Your Dog' (1989)," originally performed on *Night Music*, November 26, 1989, YouTube video, 2:55, https://www.youtube.com/watch?v=EWdz8_uQhHE; "Nirvana—'I Wanna Be Your Dog' (High Quality)," loose cover, recorded live on December 3, 1989, YouTube video, 4:51, https://www.youtube.com/watch?v=q59US9Oe220 (note "Now I wanna some marijuana" three minutes in); details of Roseland show here: "Live Nirvana

Concert Chronology: November 15, 1993—Roseland Ballroom, New York, NY, US," Live-Nirvana.com, https://www.livenirvana.com/concerts/93/93-11-15.php (accessed November 3, 2022); almost-listenable audio of the "I Wanna Be Your Dog" performance: "The Legend! w/ Nirvana and Jad Fair—'I Wanna Be Your Dog,'" performed at Roseland, November 15, 1993, YouTube video, 3:08, https://www.youtube.com/watch?v=8oOnMTfYdk4; and "R.E.M., Patti Smith Perform 'I Wanna Be Your Dog' at the March 12, 2007 [Rock and Roll Hall of Fame] Induction Ceremony," YouTube video, 3:34, https://www.youtube.com/watch?v=yUyNLASupDk.

5. See Moore, *Sells Like Teen Spirit*—or just watch near the end of the grunge documentary *Hype!* (dir. Doug Pray, Cinepix, 1996) where Bruce Pavitt and Jonathan Poneman wave at new skyscrapers in the Seattle landscape and jokingly take credit for them.

6. Hicks, *Sixties Rock*; and Smith, *Just Kids*.

7. Muñoz, *Disidentifications*.

8. Brown, *Godfather of Soul*, 138.

9. Cockrell, *Demons of Disorder*, 79.

10. See, for example, Marcus, *In the Fascist Bathroom*, 359.

11. Tosches, *Where Dead Voices Gather*; and Cantwell, *When We Were Good*.

12. Lipsitz, "'Ain't Nobody Here but Us Chickens,'" in *Rainbow at Midnight*, 327.

13. Baraka [Jones], *Blues People*, 164–65.

14. Amanda Hatfield, "*Maximum Rocknroll* to 'Pause' Publishing White Writers (unless They Are Covering POC)," *Brooklyn Vegan*, September 10, 2020.

## Outro

1. Jacqueline Zeisloft, "On *Clean*, Soccer Mommy Showcases How Disillusionment Can Lead to Growth," *Nashville Scene*, March 1, 2018, https://www.nashvillescene.com/music/features/article/20994028/on-clean-soccer-mommy-showcases-how-disillusionment-can-lead-to-growth.

# BIBLIOGRAPHY


Abbott, Lynn, and Doug Seroff. *Ragged but Right: Black Traveling Shows, "Coon Songs," and the Dark Pathway to Blues and Jazz*. Jackson: University Press of Mississippi, 2007.

Ake, David. *Jazz Cultures*. Berkeley: University of California Press, 2002.

Bangs, Lester. "Where Were You When Elvis Died?" In *Psychotic Reactions and Carburetor Dung*, edited by Greil Marcus, 212–16. New York: Knopf, 1987. Originally published as "How Long Will We Care?," *Village Voice*, August 29, 1977.

Baraka, Amiri [LeRoi Jones]. *Blues People: Negro Music in White America*. New York: William Morrow, 1963.

Barnett, Kyle. *Record Cultures: The Transformation of the U.S. Recording Industry*. Ann Arbor: University of Michigan Press, 2020.

Beatles, The. *The Beatles Anthology*. San Francisco: Chronicle, 2000.

Bertrand, Michael T. *Race, Rock, and Elvis*. Urbana: University of Illinois Press, 2000.

Blesh, Rudi. *Shining Trumpets: A History of Jazz*. 2nd ed. New York: Knopf, 1958.

Booth, Stanley. "Situation Report: Elvis in Memphis, 1967." In *Rythm Oil: A Journey through the Music of the American South*, 49–64, 182–83. New York: Vintage, 1993. Originally published as "A Hound Dog to the Manor Born."

Booth, Stanley. *The True Adventures of the Rolling Stones*. New York: Random House, 1984. Originally published under the title *Dance with the Devil: The Rolling Stones and Their Times*.

Brooks, Daphne A. *Liner Notes for the Revolution: The Intellectual Life of Black Feminist Sound*. Cambridge, MA: Harvard University Press, 2021.

Broven, John. *Record Makers and Breakers: Voices of the Independent Rock 'n' Roll*

*Pioneers*. Urbana: University of Illinois Press, 2009.

Brown, James. *James Brown, the Godfather of Soul*. With Bruce Tucker. New York: Macmillan, 1986.

Bruno, Franklin. "'Is That All There Is?' and the Uses of Disenchantment." In *Listen Again: A Momentary History of Pop Music*, edited by Eric Weisbard, 137–49. Durham, NC: Duke University Press, 2007.

Burford, Mark. *Mahalia Jackson and the Gospel Field*. New York: Oxford University Press, 2018.

Cantwell, Robert. *When We Were Good: The Folk Revival*. Cambridge, MA: Harvard University Press, 1996.

Charters, Samuel. *Elvis Presley Calls His Mother after the Ed Sullivan Show: A Novel*. Minneapolis: Coffee House, 1992.

Cockrell, Dale. *Demons of Disorder: Early Blackface Minstrels and Their World*. New York: Cambridge University Press, 1997.

Cohen, Harvey. *Duke Ellington's America*. Chicago: University of Chicago Press, 2010.

Cohn, Nik. *Awopbopaloobop Alopbamboom: The Golden Age of Rock*. New York: Da Capo, 1996. Also published under the titles *Pop from the Beginning* (1969), *Rock from the Beginning* (1969), and *Awopbopaloobop Alopbamboom: Pop from the Beginning* (1970).

Comentale, Edward. *Sweet Air: Modernism, Regionalism, and American Popular Song*. Urbana: University of Illinois Press, 2013.

Cruz, Jon. *Culture on the Margins: The Black Spiritual and the Rise of American Cultural Interpretation*. Princeton, NJ: Princeton University Press, 1999.

Daniel, Pete. *Lost Revolutions: The South in the 1950s*. Chapel Hill: University of North Carolina Press, 2000.

Davies, Hunter. *The Beatles: The Authorized Biography*. New York: McGraw-Hill, 1968.

Decker, Todd. *Who Should Sing "Ol' Man River"? The Lives of an American Song*. New York: Oxford University Press, 2014.

DeLillo, Don. *Great Jones Street*. Boston: Houghton Mifflin, 1973.

DeLillo, Don. *White Noise*. New York: Viking, 1985.

Denning, Michael. *The Cultural Front: The Laboring of American Culture in the Twentieth Century*. New York: Verso, 1996.

Denning, Michael. *Noise Uprising: The Audiopolitics of a World Musical Revolution*. New York: Verso, 2015.

DeVeaux, Scott. *The Birth of Bebop: A Social and Musical History*. Berkeley: University of California Press, 1997.

Dore, Florence. *Novel Sounds: Southern Fiction in the Age of Rock and Roll*. New York: Columbia University Press, 2018.

Dylan, Bob. *Chronicles*. Vol. 1. New York: Simon and Schuster, 2004.

Eberly, Philip K. *Music in the Air: America's Changing Tastes in Popular Music, 1920–1980*. New York: Hastings House, 1982.

Edwards, Brent Hayes. "The Literary Ellington." In *Uptown Conversation: The New Jazz Studies*, edited by Robert O'Meally, Brent Hayes Edwards, and Farah Jasmine Griffin, 326–56. New York: Columbia University Press, 2004.

Eidsheim, Nina Sun. *The Race of Sound: Listening, Timbre, and Vocality in African American Music*. Durham, NC: Duke University Press, 2015.

Ellison, Harlan. *Rockabilly*. New York: Fawcett Gold Medal, 1961. Subsequently republished under the title *Spider Kiss*.

Ellison, Ralph. *Invisible Man*. New York: Random House, 1952.

Ennis, Philip H. *The Seventh Stream: The Emergence of Rocknroll in American Popular Music*. Middletown, CT: Wesleyan University Press, 1992.

Erenberg, Lewis. *Swingin' the Dream: Big Band Jazz and the Rebirth of American Culture*. Chicago: University of Chicago Press, 1998.

Fink, Robert. "Elvis Everywhere: Musicology and Popular Music Studies at the Twilight of the Canon." *American Music* 16, no. 2 (Summer 1998): 135–79.

Gelatt, Roland. *The Fabulous Phonograph: From Tin-Foil to High Fidelity*. Philadelphia: J. B. Lippincott, 1955. 2nd rev. ed., New York: Macmillan, 1977.

Giddins, Gary. *Bing Crosby*. Vol. 1, *A Pocketful of Dreams: The Early Years, 1903–1940*. Boston: Little, Brown, 2001.

Giddins, Gary. *Bing Crosby*. Vol. 2, *Swinging on a Star: The War Years, 1940–1946*. Boston: Little, Brown, 2018.

Giddins, Gary. "The Whiteness of the Wail." In *Riding on a Blue Note: Jazz and American Pop*, 252–57. New York: Oxford University Press, 1981. Originally published in the *Village Voice*, July 1977.

Gilbert, David. *The Product of Our Souls: Ragtime, Race, and the Birth of the Manhattan Musical Marketplace*. Chapel Hill: University of North Carolina Press, 2016.

Gillett, Charlie. *The Sound of the City: The Rise of Rock and Roll*. New York: Outerbridge and Dienstfrey, 1970. Rev. ed., New York: Pantheon, 1984.

Goldman, Albert. *Elvis*. New York: McGraw Hill, 1981.

Graham, Sandra Jean. *Spirituals and the Birth of a Black Entertainment Industry*. Urbana: University of Illinois Press, 2018.

Gregory, James N. *The Southern Diaspora: How the Great Migrations of Black and White Southerners Transformed America*. Chapel Hill: University of North Carolina Press, 2005.

Guralnick, Peter. "Elvis Presley." In *The Rolling Stone Illustrated History of Rock and Roll*, edited by Jim Miller, 30–40. New York: Rolling Stone Press, 1976.

Guralnick, Peter. *Feel Like Going Home: Portraits in Blues, Country, and Rock 'n' Roll*. New York: Outerbridge and Dienstfrey, 1971.

Guralnick, Peter. *Last Train to Memphis: The Rise of Elvis Presley*. Boston: Little, Brown, 1994.

Guralnick, Peter. *Lost Highway: Journeys and Arrivals of American Musicians*. Boston: David R. Godine, 1979.

Halberstam, Jack. *Female Masculinity*. Durham, NC: Duke University Press, 1998.

Halberstam, Jack. "Queer Voices and Musical Genders." In *Oh Boy! Masculinities in Popular Music*, edited by Freya Jarman-Ivens, 183–95. New York: Routledge, 2007.

Hale, Grace Elizabeth. *Cool Town: How Athens, Georgia, Launched Alternative Music and Changed American Culture*. Chapel Hill: University of North Carolina Press, 2020.

Hall, Stuart, and Tony Jefferson, eds. *Resistance through Rituals: Youth Subcultures in Post-war Britain*. London: Hutchinson, 1976.

Hamilton, Marybeth. *In Search of the Blues*. New York: Basic Books, 2008.

Handy, W. C. *Father of the Blues: An Autobiography*. New York: Macmillan, 1941.

Hebdige, Dick. *Subculture: The Meaning of Style*. London: Methuen, 1979.

Hersch, Charles. *Subversive Sounds: Race and the Birth of Jazz in New Orleans*. Chicago: University of Chicago Press, 2007.

Hicks, Michael. *Sixties Rock: Garage, Psychedelic, and Other Satisfactions*. Urbana: University of Illinois Press, 2000.

Hilmes, Michele. *Only Connect: A Cultural History of Broadcasting in the United States*. 4th ed. Belmont, CA: Wadsworth/Cengage, 2014.

Hopkins, Jerry. *Elvis: A Biography*. New York: Simon and Schuster, 1971. Subsequently republished under the title *Elvis: The Biography*.

Huber, Patrick. *Linthead Stomp: The Creation of Country Music in the Piedmont South*.

Chapel Hill: University of North Carolina Press, 2008.

Hunter, Tera W. "'Sexual Pantomimes,' the Blues Aesthetic and Black Women in the New South." In *Music and the Racial Imagination*, edited by Ronald Radano and Philip Bohlman, 145–64. Chicago: University of Chicago Press, 2000.

John, Elton. *Me: Elton John*. New York: Henry Holt, 2019.

Johnson, Robert. *Elvis Presley Speaks!* New York: Rave, 1956.

Kahn, E. J., Jr. *The Voice: The Story of an American Phenomenon*. New York: Harper and Brothers, 1947.

Kaplan, James. *Frank: The Voice*. New York: Doubleday, 2010.

Katz, Mark. *Capturing Sound: How Technology Has Changed Music*. Berkeley: University of California Press, 2005.

Kaye, Lenny. *You Call It Madness: The Sensuous Song of the Croon*. New York: Villard, 2004.

Keightley, Keir. "Long Play: Oriented Popular Music and the Temporal Logics of the Postwar Sound Recording Industry in the USA." *Media, Culture and Society* 26, no. 3 (2004): 375–91.

Keightley, Keir. "Music for Middlebrows: Defining the Easy Listening Era, 1946–1966." *American Music* 26, no. 3 (2008): 309–35.

Keightley, Keir. "'You Keep Coming Back Like a Song': Adult Audiences, Taste Panics, and the Idea of the Standard." *Journal of Popular Music Studies* 13, no. 1 (March 2001): 7–40.

Kenney, William Howland. *Recorded Music in American Life: The Phonograph and Popular Memory, 1890–1940*. New York: Oxford University Press, 1999.

Knapp, Raymond, Mitchell Morris, and Stacy Wolf, eds. *The Oxford Handbook of the American Musical*. New York: Oxford University Press, 2011.

Kun, Josh. *Audiotopia: Music, Race, and America*. Berkeley: University of California Press, 2005.

Lange, Jeffrey J. *Smile When You Call Me a Hillbilly: Country Music's Struggle for Respectability, 1939–1954*. Athens: University of Georgia Press, 2004.

Leiber, Jerry, and Mike Stoller. *Hound Dog: The Leiber and Stoller Autobiography*. With David Ritz. New York: Simon and Schuster, 2009.

Lennon, John, and Yoko Ono. *All We Are Saying: The Last Major Interview with John Lennon and Yoko Ono*. Interview by David

Sheff. Edited by G. Barry Golson. New York: St. Martin's, 2000.

Lhamon, W. T., Jr. *Jump Jim Crow: Lost Plays, Lyrics, and Street Prose of the First Atlantic Popular Culture*. Cambridge, MA: Harvard University Press, 2003.

Lhamon, W. T., Jr. *Raising Cain: Blackface Performance from Jim Crow to Hip Hop*. Cambridge, MA: Harvard University Press, 1998.

Lipsitz, George. "Introduction." In Johnny Otis, *Upside Your Head! Rhythm and Blues on Central Avenue*, xvii–xxxv. Hanover, NH: University Press of New England, 1993.

Lipsitz, George. *Midnight at the Barrelhouse: The Johnny Otis Story*. Minneapolis: University of Minnesota Press, 2013.

Lipsitz, George. *Rainbow at Midnight: Labor and Culture in the 1940s*. Urbana: University of Illinois Press, 1994.

Lott, Eric. *Love and Theft: Blackface Minstrelsy and the American Working Class*. New York: Oxford University Press, 1993.

Mack, Kimberly. *Fictional Blues: Narrative Self-Invention from Bessie Smith to Jack White*. Amherst: University of Massachusetts Press, 2020.

Mackey, Nathaniel. "Other: From Noun to Verb." *Representations*, no. 39 (Summer 1992): 51–70.

Mahon, Maureen. *Black Diamond Queens: African American Women and Rock and Roll*. Durham, NC: Duke University Press, 2021.

Mahon, Maureen. "Listening for Willie Mae 'Big Mama' Thornton's Voice: The Sound of Race and Gender Transgressions in Rock and Roll." *Women and Music: A Journal of Gender and Culture* 15, no. 1 (January 2011): 1–17.

Mailer, Norman. "The White Negro: Superficial Reflections on the Hipster." *Dissent* (Fall 1957): 276–93.

Malone, Bill C. *Country Music USA*. With Tracy E. W. Laird. 50th anniv. ed. Austin: University of Texas Press, 2018.

Marcus, Greil. *Dead Elvis: A Chronicle of a Cultural Obsession*. Cambridge, MA: Harvard University Press, 1999.

Marcus, Greil. *Double Trouble: Bill Clinton and Elvis Presley in a Land of No Alternatives*. New York: Henry Holt, 2001.

Marcus, Greil. *In the Fascist Bathroom: Punk and Pop Music, 1977–1992*. Cambridge, MA: Harvard University Press, 1993.

Marcus, Greil. *Like a Rolling Stone: Bob Dylan at the Crossroads*. New York: Public Affairs, 2006.

Marcus, Greil. *Mystery Train: Images of America in Rock 'n' Roll Music*. 1975. London: Folio Society, 2020.

Marcus, Greil. *Real Life Rock: The Complete Top Ten Columns, 1986–2014*. New Haven, CT: Yale University Press, 2015.

Maslon, Laurence. *Broadway to Main Street: How Show Tunes Enchanted America*. New York: Oxford University Press, 2018.

Mast, Gerald. *Can't Help Singin': The American Musical on Stage and Screen*. Woodstock, NY: Overlook, 1987.

Mazor, Barry. *Meeting Jimmie Rodgers: How America's Original Roots Music Hero Changed the Pop Sounds of a Century*. New York: Oxford University Press, 2009.

McCracken, Allison. *Real Men Don't Sing: Crooning in American Culture*. Durham, NC: Duke University Press, 2015.

McGinley, Paige. *Staging the Blues: From Tent Shows to Tourism*. Durham, NC: Duke University Press, 2014.

McKee, Margaret, and Fred Chisenhall. *Beale Black and Blue: Life and Music on Black America's Main Street*. Baton Rouge: Louisiana State University Press, 1993.

McRobbie, Angela. "Settling Accounts with Subculture: A Feminist Critique." *Screen Education* 34 (Spring 1980): 37–49.

Miller, Karl Hagstrom. *Segregating Sound: Inventing Folk and Pop Music in the Age of Jim Crow*. Durham, NC: Duke University Press, 2010.

Moore, Ryan. *Sells Like Teen Spirit: Music, Youth Culture, and Social Crisis*. New York: New York University Press, 2010.

Most, Andrea. *Making Americans: Jews and the Broadway Musical*. Cambridge, MA: Harvard University Press, 2004.

Moten, Fred. *In the Break: The Aesthetics of the Black Radical Tradition*. Minneapolis: University of Minnesota Press, 2003.

Muñoz, José Esteban. *Disidentifications: Queers of Color and the Performance of Politics*. Minneapolis: University of Minnesota Press, 1999.

Neal, Jocelyn. *The Songs of Jimmie Rodgers: A Legacy in Country Music*. Bloomington: Indiana University Press, 2009.

Otis, Johnny. *Listen to the Lambs*. New York: W. W. Norton, 1968.

Otis, Johnny. *Upside Your Head! Rhythm and Blues on Central Avenue*. Hanover, NH: University Press of New England, 1993.

Page, Patti. "There Are Two Sides to a Song." *Music Journal*, March 1960, 16.

Page, Patti. *This Is My Song: A Memoir*. With Skip Press. Bath, NH: Kathdan, 2009.

Palmer, Robert. *Blues and Chaos: The Music Writing of Robert Palmer*. Edited by Anthony DeCurtis. New York: Scribner, 2009.

Palmer, Robert. "The Church of the Sonic Guitar." *South Atlantic Quarterly* 90, no. 4 (Fall 1991): 649–73.

Palmer, Robert. *Rock and Roll: An Unruly History*. New York: Harmony Books, 1995.

Peellaert, Guy, and Nik Cohn. *Rock Dreams*. New York: Popular Library, 1973.

Peterson, Richard. "Why 1955? Explaining the Advent of Rock Music." *Popular Music* 9, no. 1 (1990): 97–116.

Petkov, Steven, and Leonard Mustazza, eds. *The Frank Sinatra Reader*. New York: Oxford University Press, 1995.

Radano, Ronald. *Lying Up a Nation: Race and Black Music*. Chicago: University of Chicago Press, 2003.

Ramsey, Guthrie, Jr. *Race Music: Black Cultures from Bebop to Hip-Hop*. Berkeley: University of California Press, 2004.

Richards, Keith. *Life*. With James Fox. Boston: Little, Brown, 2010.

Rodman, Gilbert. *Elvis after Elvis: The Posthumous Career of a Living Legend*. New York: Routledge, 1996.

Rogin, Michael. *Blackface, White Noise: Jewish Immigrants and the Hollywood Melting Pot*. Berkeley: University of California Press, 1996.

Salem, James M. *The Late Great Johnny Ace and the Transition from R&B to Rock 'n' Roll*. Urbana: University of Illinois Press, 2001.

Sanjek, Russell. *Pennies from Heaven: The American Popular Music Business in the Twentieth Century*. Updated by David Sanjek. New York: Da Capo, 1996.

Schoemer, Karen. *Great Pretenders: My Strange Love Affair with '50s Pop Music*. New York: Free Press, 2006.

Shaw, Arnold. *The World of Soul: Black America's Contribution to the Pop Music Scene*. New York: Cowles, 1970.

Small, Christopher. *Musicking: The Meanings of Performing and Listening*. Middletown, CT: Wesleyan University Press, 1998.

Smith, Patti. *Just Kids*. New York: Ecco, 2010.

Spörke, Michael. *Big Mama Thornton: The Life and Music*. Jefferson, NC: McFarland, 2014.

Springsteen, Bruce. *Born to Run*. New York: Simon and Schuster, 2016.

Stearns, Marshall. *The Story of Jazz*. New York: Oxford University Press, 1956.

Stearns, Marshall, and Jean Stearns. *Jazz Dance: The Story of American Vernacular Dance*. New York: Macmillan, 1968.

Steptoe, Tyina. "Big Mama Thornton, Little Richard, and the Queer Roots of Rock 'n' Roll." *American Quarterly* 70, no. 1 (March 2018): 55–77.

Steptoe, Tyina. "Jody's Got Your Girl and Gone: Gender, Folklore, and the Black Working Class." *Journal of African American History* 99, no. 3 (2014): 251–74.

Stimeling, Travis, ed. *The Oxford Handbook of Country Music*. New York: Oxford University Press, 2017.

Thompson, Edward. *The Making of the English Working Class*. New York: Pantheon, 1964.

Tosches, Nick. *Where Dead Voices Gather*. Boston: Little, Brown, 2001.

Tucker, Mark, ed. *The Duke Ellington Reader*. New York: Oxford University Press, 1993.

Vogel, Shane. *The Scene of Harlem Cabaret: Race, Sexuality, Performance*. Chicago: University of Chicago Press, 2009.

Waksman, Steve. *Instruments of Desire: The Electric Guitar and the Shaping of Musical Experience*. Cambridge, MA: Harvard University Press, 1999.

Waksman, Steve. *This Ain't the Summer of Love: Conflict and Crossover in Heavy Metal and Punk*. Berkeley: University of California Press, 2009.

Wald, Elijah. *How the Beatles Destroyed Rock 'n' Roll: An Alternative History of American Popular Music*. New York: Oxford University Press, 2011.

Wald, Gayle. "'Have a Little Talk': Listening to the B-Side of History." *Popular Music* 24, no. 3 (2005): 323–37.

Walker, Alice. "Nineteen Fifty-Five." In *You Can't Keep a Good Woman Down*, 3–20. New York: Harcourt Brace Jovanovich, 1981.

Wayne, Jane Ellen. *The Leading Men of MGM*. New York: Carroll and Graf, 2005.

Weheliye, Alexander. *Phonographies: Grooves in Sonic Afro-Modernity*. Durham, NC: Duke University Press, 2005.

Weisbard, Eric. *Songbooks: The Literature of American Music*. Durham, NC: Duke University Press, 2021.

Weisbard, Eric. *Top 40 Democracy: The Rival Mainstreams of American Music*. Chicago: University of Chicago Press, 2014.

Wenner, Jann S. *Lennon Remembers*. New ed. New York: Verso, 2000.

Yagoda, Ben. *The B Side: The Death of Tin Pan Alley and the Rebirth of the Great American Song*. New York: Riverhead Books, 2015.

Young, Kevin. *The Grey Album: On the Blackness of Blackness*. Minneapolis: Graywolf, 2012.

Zak, Albin J., III. *I Don't Sound Like Nobody: Remaking Music in 1950s America*. Ann Arbor: University of Michigan Press, 2012.

# INDEX